The American Titanic Inquiry
Inquiry
Day 1

The American Titanic Inquiry

Day 1

Titanic Researchers

All the text in this book is the record of the Committee on Commerce hearings for the Titanic disaster, which were presided over by Senator William Alden Smith.

This record can be found at US National Archives (Access and Use unrestricted) under the following title: Senate Document No. 726 "Titanic" Disaster: Hearings before the Subcommittee of the Committee on Commerce United States Senate

https://catalog.archives.gov/id/2124512

First Printing: 2018

ISBN 978-0-244-66015-4

Why this book?

A group of serious Titanic researchers has gone to the incredible effort of transcribing the entire texts of the US Senate and the British Titanic Inquiries and has graciously seen fit to post those transcripts on the website http://www.titanicinquiry.org for the benefit of Titanic buffs everywhere.

These researchers have undertaken this project solely in the interest of making hard-to-find historical information available to everyone who might wish to see it.

It gives me great pleasure to make the names of these researchers:

Bob Bonnell – CAN, Stuart Partridge – UK, Earl Chapman – CAN, Marilyn Powell – US, Mike Disabato – US, Susie Powell – US, Vera & John Gillespie – US, Parks Stephenson – US, Linda Greaves – US, Bruce Trinque – US, Jane Hilbert – US, Bill Wormstedt – US, Robert Ottmers – US ang Georges BEHE – US.

They deserve the sincere gratitude of Titanic researchers the world over.

As Titanic passionnate and searcher, I was frustrated that I could not hold their incredible work on paper or Ebook. Consequently, I decided to layout and print, as a book, this work. This is why this book exists.

Alexis Dana, Paris, France, January 10, 2018
For any comments regarding this book, do not hesitate to contact me at: alexis.danatitanic@gmail.com

How to navigate through the books?

The original Senate (US) document contains 1,683 pages. It was, of course, not possible to publish all the testimonies in one book. We decided to divide books per day.

The reader looking for a specific day or testimony can use the following :

Day 1
> Joseph B. Ismay
> Arthur H Rostron
> Guglielmo Marconi
> Charles Lightoller
> Harold T. Cottam
> Alfred Crawford

Day 2
> Harold Cottam
> Harold Bride
> Harold Cottam
> Harold Bride
> Herbert Pitman

Day 3
> Phillip Franklin
> Joseph Boxhall

Day 4
> Herbert Pitman
> Frederick Fleet
> Arthur Peuchen

Day 5
> Frederick Fleet
> Harold G. Lowe
> Charles Lightoller
> Robert Hichens

Day 6

        Guglielmo Marconi
        Harold Cottam
        Guglielmo Marconi

Day 7

        24 testimonies of Titanic crewmen

Day 8

        Phillip Franklin
        Ernest Gill
        Stanley Lord
        Cyril Evans
        Frank Evans

Day 9

        Charles Lightoller
        James Moore
        Charles Lightoller
        Phillip Franklin
        Andrew Cunningham
        Frederick Ray
        Henry Etches
        William Burke
        Alfred Crawford
        Arthur Bright
        Alfred Crawford

Day 10

        Guglielmo Marconi
        Frederick Sammis
        Hugh Woolner
        Harold Bride
        Joseph Boxhall
        Harold Cottam
        Joseph Boxhall

Day 11

        Edward Dunn

        Charles Morgan

        Joseph B. Ismay

        C. E. Stengel

        Joseph B. Ismay

        S. C. Neale

        Archibald Gracie

        Helen Bishop

        Dickinson Bishop

        Archibald Gracie

Day 12

        Mrs. J. Stuart White

        John Bottomley

Day 13

        Daniel Buckley

        Melville Stone

        George Harder

        John Binns

        Olaus Abelseth

        Norman Chambers

Day 14

        Frederick Dauler

        Harold Bride

        Berk Pickard

        Gilbert Balfour

Day 15

        Maurice Farrell

Day 16

        Benjamin Campbell

Day 17

        John J. Knapp

Day 18

        Herbert Haddock

        E. J. Moore

        Frederick Barrett

Contents

TESTIMONY OF Mr. J. BRUCE ISMAY.

Managing Director, I.M.M. (White Star Line); First Class
Passenger, SS Titanic

Mr. J. Bruce Ismay, being duly sworn by the chairman, testified as follows:

Senator SMITH. Mr. Ismay, for the purpose of simplifying this hearing, I will ask you a few preliminary questions.

First state your full name, please?

Mr. ISMAY. Joseph Bruce Ismay.

Senator SMITH. And your place of residence?

Mr. ISMAY. Liverpool.

Senator SMITH. And your age?

Mr. ISMAY. I shall be 50 on the 12th of December.

Senator SMITH. And your occupation?

Mr. ISMAY. Ship owner.

Senator SMITH. Are you an officer of the White Star Line?

Mr. ISMAY. I am.

Senator SMITH. In what capacity?

Mr. ISMAY. Managing Director.

Senator SMITH. As such officer, were you officially designated to make the trial trip of the Titanic?

Mr. ISMAY. No.

Senator SMITH. Were you a voluntary passenger?

Mr. ISMAY. A voluntary passenger, yes.

Senator SMITH. Where did you board the ship?

Mr. ISMAY. At Southampton.

Senator SMITH. At what time?

Mr. ISMAY. I think it was 9.30 in the morning.

Senator SMITH. Of what day?

Mr. Ismay. The 10th of April.

Senator SMITH. The port of destination was New York?

Mr. ISMAY. New York.

Senator SMITH. Will you kindly tell the committee the circumstances surrounding your voyage, and, as succinctly as possible, beginning with your going aboard the vessel at Liverpool, your place on the ship on the voyage, together with any circumstances you feel would be helpful to us in this inquiry?

Mr. ISMAY. In the first place, I would like to express my sincere grief at this deplorable catastrophe.

I understand that you gentlemen have been appointed as a committee of the Senate to inquire into the circumstances. So far as we are concerned, we welcome it. We court the fullest inquiry. We have nothing to conceal; nothing to hide. The ship was built in Belfast. She was the latest thing in the art of shipbuilding; absolutely no money was spared in her construction. She was not built by contract. She was simply built on a commission.

She left Belfast, as far as I remember - I am not absolutely clear about these dates - I think it was on the 1st of April.

She underwent her trials, which were entirely satisfactory. She then proceeded to Southampton; arriving there on Wednesday.

Senator SMITH. Will you describe the trials she went through ?

Mr. ISMAY. I was not present.

She arrived at Southampton on Wednesday, the 3d, I think, and sailed on Wednesday, the 10th. She left Southampton at 12 o'clock.

She arrived in Cherbourg that evening, having run over at 68 revolutions.

We left Cherbourg and proceeded to Queenstown. We arrived there, I think, about midday on Thursday.

We ran from Cherbourg to Queenstown at 70 revolutions.

After embarking the mails and passengers, we proceeded at 70 revolutions. I am not absolutely clear what the first day's run was, whether it was 464 miles or 484 miles.

The second day the number of revolutions was increased. I think the number of revolutions on the second day was about 72. I think we ran on the second day 519 miles.

The third day the revolutions were increased to 75, and I think we ran 546 or 549 miles.

The weather during this time was absolutely fine, with the exception, I think, of about 10 minutes' fog one evening.

The accident took place on Sunday night. What the exact time was I do not know. I was in bed myself, asleep, when the accident happened.

The ship sank, I am told, at 2:20.

That, sir, I think is all I can tell you.

I understand it has been stated that the ship was going at full speed. The ship never had been at full speed. The full speed of the ship is 78 revolutions. She works up to 80. So far as I am aware, she never exceeded 75 revolutions. She had not all her boilers on. None of the single-ended boilers were on.

It was our intention, if we had fine weather on Monday afternoon or Tuesday, to drive the ship at full speed. That, owing to the unfortunate catastrophe, never eventuated.

Senator SMITH. Will you describe what you did after the impact or collision?

Mr. ISMAY. I presume the impact awakened me. I lay in bed for a moment or two afterwards, not realizing, probably, what had happened. Eventually I got up and walked along the passageway and met one of the stewards, and said, "What has happened?" He said, "I do not know, sir."

I then went back into my room, put my coat on, and went up on the bridge, where I found Capt. Smith. I asked him what had happened, and he said, "We have struck ice." I said, "Do you think the ship is seriously damaged?" He said, "I am afraid she is."

I then went down below, I think it was, where I met Mr. Bell, the chief engineer, who was in the main companionway. I asked if he thought the ship was seriously damaged, and he said he thought she was, but was quite satisfied the pumps would keep her afloat.

I think I went back onto the bridge. I heard the order given to get the boats out. I walked along to the starboard side of the ship, where I met one of the officers. I told him to get the boats out -

Senator SMITH. What officer?

Mr. ISMAY. That I could not remember, sir.

I assisted, as best I could, getting the boats out and putting the women and children into the boats.

I stood upon that deck practically until I left the ship in the starboard collapsible boat, which is the last boat to leave the ship, so far as I know. More than that I do not know.

Senator SMITH. Did the captain remain on the bridge?

Mr. ISMAY. That I could not tell you, sir.

Senator SMITH. Did you leave him on the bridge?

Mr. ISMAY. Yes, sir.

Senator SMITH. His first statement to you was that he felt she was seriously damaged?

Mr. ISMAY. Yes, sir.

Senator SMITH. And the next statement of the chief engineer was what?

Mr. ISMAY. To the same effect.

Senator SMITH. To the same effect?

Mr. ISMAY. Yes.

Senator SMITH. But that he hoped the pumps might keep her afloat?

Mr. ISMAY. Yes.

Senator SMITH. Did you have any talk with any officer other than the captain or the chief engineer and the steward that you met?

Mr. ISMAY. Not that I remember.

Senator SMITH. Did the officers seem to know the serious character of this collision?

Mr. ISMAY. That I could not tell, sir, because I had no conversation with them.

Senator SMITH. Did any officer say to you that it evidently was not serious?

Mr. ISMAY. No, sir.

Senator SMITH. All the officers with whom you talked expressed the same fear, saying that it was serious?

Mr. ISMAY. I did not speak to any of them, sir.

Senator SMITH. Except the captain?

Mr. ISMAY. Except the captain and the chief engineer. I have already stated that I had spoken to them; but to no other officer that I remember.

Senator SMITH. You went to the bridge immediately after you had returned to your room?

Mr. ISMAY. After I had put on my coat I went up to the bridge.

Senator SMITH. And you found the captain there?

Mr. ISMAY. The captain was there.

Senator SMITH. In what part of the ship were your quarters?

Mr. ISMAY. My quarters were on B deck, just aft of the main companionway.

Senator SMITH. I wish you would describe just where that was.

Mr. ISMAY. The sun deck is the upper deck of all. Then we have what we call the A deck, which is the next deck, and then the B deck.

Mr. UHLER. The second passenger deck?

Mr. ISMAY. We carry very few passengers on the A deck. I think we have a diagram here that will show you these decks. Here it is, and there is the room I was occupying [indicating on diagram].

Senator SMITH. What is the number of that room?

Mr. ISMAY. B-52 is the room I had.

Senator SMITH. You had the suite?

Mr. ISMAY. I had the suite; I was sleeping in that room [indicating on diagram], as a matter of fact.

Senator SMITH. Do you know whether there were any passengers on that deck?

Mr. ISMAY. I have no idea, sir.

Senator SMITH. You say that the trip was a voluntary trip on your part?

Mr. ISMAY. Absolutely.

Senator SMITH. For the purpose of viewing this ship in action, or did you have some business in New York?

Mr. ISMAY. I had no business to bring me to New York at all. I simply came in the natural course of events, as one is apt to, in the case of a new ship, to see how she works, and with the idea of seeing how we could improve on her for the next ship which we are building.

Senator SMITH. Were there any other executive officers of the company aboard?

Mr. ISMAY. None.

Senator SMITH. Was the inspector or builder on board?

Mr. ISMAY. There was a representative of the builders on board.

Senator SMITH. Who was he?

Mr. ISMAY. Mr. Thomas Andrews.

Senator SMITH. In what capacity was he?

Mr. ISMAY. I do not quite follow you.

Senator SMITH. What was the occasion of his coming to make this trial trip?

Mr. ISMAY. As a representative of the builders, to see that everything was working satisfactorily and also to see how he could improve the next ship.

Senator SMITH. Was he a man of large experience?

Mr. ISMAY. Yes.

Senator SMITH. Had he had part in the construction of this ship himself?

Mr. ISMAY. Yes.

Senator SMITH. Was he among the survivors?

Mr. ISMAY. Unfortunately, no.

Senator SMITH. How old a man was he?

Mr. ISMAY. It is difficult to judge a man's age, as you know, but I should think he was perhaps 42 or 43 years of age. He may have been less. I really could not say.

Senator SMITH. Then, you were the only executive officer aboard representing your company, aside from the ship's customary complement of officers?

Mr. ISMAY. Yes, sir.

Senator SMITH. Did you have occasion to consult with the captain about the movement of the ship? Mr. ISMAY. Never.

Senator SMITH. Did he consult you about it?

Mr. ISMAY. Never. Perhaps I am wrong in saying that. I should like to say this: I do not know that it was quite a matter of consulting him about it, of his consulting me about it, but what we had arranged to do was that we would not attempt to arrive in New York at the lightship before 5 o'clock on Wednesday morning.

Senator SMITH. That was the understanding?

Mr. ISMAY. Yes. But that was arranged before we left Queenstown.

Senator SMITH. Was it supposed that you could reach New York at that time without putting the ship to its full running capacity?

Mr. ISMAY. Oh, yes, sir. There was nothing to be gained by arriving at New York any earlier than that.

Senator SMITH. You spoke of the revolutions on the early part of the voyage.

Mr. ISMAY. Yes, sir.

Senator SMITH. Those were increased as the distance was increased?

Mr. ISMAY. The Titanic being a new ship, we were gradually working her up. When you bring out a new ship you naturally do not start her running at full speed until you get everything working smoothly and satisfactorily down below.

Senator SMITH. Did I understand you to say that she exceeded 70 revolutions?

Mr. ISMAY. Yes, sir; she was going 75 revolutions on Tuesday.

Senator SMITH. On Tuesday?

Mr. ISMAY. No; I am wrong - on Saturday. I am mixed up as to the days.

Senator SMITH. The day before the accident?

Mr. ISMAY. The day before the accident. That, of course, is nothing near her full speed.

Senator SMITH. During the voyage, do you know, of your own knowledge, of your proximity to icebergs?

Mr. ISMAY. Did I know that we were near icebergs?

Senator SMITH. Yes.

Mr. ISMAY. No, sir; I did not. I know ice had been reported.

Senator SMITH. Ice had been reported?

Mr. ISMAY. Yes.

Senator SMITH. Did you personally see any icebergs, or any large volume of ice?

Mr. ISMAY. No; not until after the accident.

Senator SMITH. Not until after the wreck?

Mr. ISMAY. I had never seen an iceberg in my life before.

Senator SMITH. You never saw one before.

Mr. ISMAY. No, sir.

Senator SMITH. Had you ever been on this so-called northern route before?

Mr. ISMAY. We were on the southern route, sir.

Senator SMITH. On this Newfoundland route?

Mr. ISMAY. We were on the long southern route; not on the northern route.

Senator SMITH. You were not on the extreme northern route?

Mr. ISMAY. We were on the extreme southern route for the west-bound ships.

Senator SMITH. What was the longitude and latitude of this ship? Do you know?

Mr. ISMAY. That I could not tell you; I am not a sailor.

Senator SMITH. Were you cognizant of your proximity to icebergs at all on Saturday?

Mr. ISMAY. On Saturday? No, sir.

Senator SMITH. Do you know anything about a wireless message from the Amerika to the Titanic -

Mr. ISMAY. No, sir.

Senator SMITH. Saying that the Amerika had encountered ice in that latitude?

Mr. ISMAY. No, sir.

Senator SMITH. Were you aware of the proximity of icebergs on Sunday?

Mr. ISMAY. On Sunday? No; I did not know on Sunday. I knew that we would be in the ice region that night sometime.

Senator SMITH. That you would be or were?

Mr. ISMAY. That we would be in the ice region on Sunday night.

Senator SMITH. Did you have any consultation with the captain regarding the matter?

Mr. ISMAY. Absolutely none.

Senator SMITH. Or with any other officer of the ship?

Mr. ISMAY. With no officer at all, sir. It was absolutely out of my province. I am not a navigator. I was simply a passenger on board the ship.

Senator SMITH. Do you know anything about the working of the wireless service on this ship?

Mr. ISMAY. In what way? We had wireless on the ship.

Senator SMITH. Had you taken any unusual precaution to have a reserve power for this wireless?

Mr. ISMAY. I believe there was, but I have no knowledge of that myself.

Senator SMITH. Do you know how long the wireless continued to operate after the blow or collision?

Mr. ISMAY. No, sir; I do not.

Senator SMITH. Did you, at any time see the operator of the wireless?

Mr. ISMAY. I did not.

Senator SMITH. Did you attempt to send any messages yourself?

Mr. ISMAY. I did not.

Senator SMITH. Were you outside on the deck, or on any deck, when the order was given to lower the lifeboats?

Mr. ISMAY. I heard Capt. Smith give the order when I was on the bridge.

Senator SMITH. You heard the captain give the order?

Mr. ISMAY. Yes, sir.

Senator SMITH. Will you tell us what he said.

Mr. ISMAY. It is very difficult for me to remember exactly what was said, sir.

Senator SMITH. As nearly as you can.

Mr. ISMAY.   I know I heard him give the order to lower the boats. I think that is all he said. I think he simply turned around and gave the order.

Senator SMITH.   Was there anything else said, as to how they should be manned or occupied?

Mr. ISMAY.   No, sir; not that I heard. As soon as I heard him give the order to lower the boats, I left the bridge.

Senator SMITH.   You left the bridge?

Mr. ISMAY.   Yes.

Senator SMITH.   Did you see any of the boats lowered?

Mr. ISMAY.   Yes, sir.

Senator SMITH.   How many?

Mr. ISMAY.   Certainly three.

Senator SMITH.   Will you tell us, if you can, how they were lowered?

Mr. ISMAY.   They were swung out, people were put into the boats from the deck, and then they were simply lowered away down to the water.

Senator SMITH.   Were these lifeboats on the various decks?

Mr. ISMAY.   They were all on one deck.

Senator SMITH.   On what deck?

Mr. ISMAY.   On the sun deck; the deck above this [indicating on diagram]. I do not think it is shown on this plan.

Senator SMITH.   That is, the second deck above yours?

Mr. ISMAY.   On this deck here, on the big plan [indicating].

Senator SMITH.   On the sun deck?

Mr. ISMAY.   Yes; on what we call the sun deck or the boat deck.

Senator SMITH. They were on the boat deck, which would be the upper deck of all?

Mr. ISMAY. The upper deck of all, yes.

Senator SMITH. Was there any order or supervision exercised by the officers of the ship in loading these lifeboats?

Mr. ISMAY. Yes, sir.

Senator SMITH. I wish you would tell just what that was.

Mr. ISMAY. That I could not say. I could only speak from what I saw for myself.

Senator SMITH. That is all I wish you to do.

Mr. ISMAY. The boats that were lowered where I was were in charge of the officer and were filled and lowered away.

Senator SMITH. They first put men into the boats for the purpose of controlling them?

Mr. ISMAY. We put in some of the ship's people.

Senator SMITH. Some of the ship's people?

Mr. ISMAY. Yes.

Senator SMITH. How many?

Mr. ISMAY. That I could not say.

Senator SMITH. About how many?

Mr. ISMAY. I could not say.

Senator SMITH. About three or four?

Mr. ISMAY. The officer who was there will be able to give you that information, sir. My own statement would be simply guesswork. His statement would be reliable.

Senator SMITH. In the boat in which you left the ship how many men were on board?

Mr. ISMAY. Four.

Senator SMITH. Besides yourself?

Mr. ISMAY. I thought you meant the crew.

Senator SMITH. I did mean the crew.

Mr. ISMAY. There were four of the crew.

Senator SMITH. What position did these men occupy?

Mr. ISMAY. I do not know, sir.

Senator SMITH. Were any of them officers?

Mr. ISMAY. No.

Senator SMITH. Or seamen?

Mr. ISMAY. I believe one was a quartermaster.

Senator SMITH. One was a quartermaster?

Mr. ISMAY. I believe so, but I do not know.

Senator SMITH. You saw three of the boats lowered yourself?

Mr. ISMAY. Yes.

Senator SMITH. And three of them loaded?

Mr. ISMAY. Yes.

Senator SMITH. As they were loaded, was any order given as to how they should be loaded?

Mr. ISMAY. No.

Senator SMITH. How did it happen that the women were first put aboard these lifeboats?

Mr. ISMAY. The natural order would be women and children first.

Senator SMITH. Was that the order?

Mr. ISMAY. Oh, yes.

Senator SMITH. That was followed?

Mr. ISMAY. As far as practicable.

Senator SMITH. So far as you observed?

Mr. ISMAY. So far as I observed.

Senator SMITH. And were all the women and children accommodated in these lifeboats?

Mr. ISMAY. I could not tell you, sir.

Senator SMITH. How many passengers were in the lifeboat in which you left the ship?

Mr. ISMAY. I should think about 45.

Senator SMITH. Forty-five?

Mr. ISMAY. That is my recollection.

Senator SMITH. Was that its full capacity?

Mr. ISMAY. Practically.

Senator SMITH. How about the other two boats?

Mr. ISMAY. The other three, I should think, were fairly loaded up.

Senator SMITH. The three besides the one you were in?

Mr. ISMAY. Yes.

Senator SMITH. They were fairly well filled?

Mr. ISMAY. Yes.

Senator SMITH. Was there any struggle or jostling?

Mr. ISMAY. I saw none.

Senator SMITH. Or any attempt by men to get into the boats?

Mr. ISMAY. I saw none.

Senator SMITH. Were these women passengers designated as they went into the lifeboat?

Mr. ISMAY. No, sir.

Senator SMITH. Those that were nearest the lifeboat were taken in?

Mr. ISMAY. We simply picked the women out and put them in the boat as fast as we could.

Senator SMITH. You picked them from among the throng?

Mr. ISMAY. We took the first ones that were there and put them in the lifeboats. I was there myself and put a lot in.

Senator SMITH. You helped put some of them in yourself?

Mr. ISMAY. I put a great many in.

Senator SMITH. Were children shown the same consideration as the women?

Mr. ISMAY. Absolutely.

Senator SMITH. Did you see any lifeboat without its complement of oarsmen?

Mr. ISMAY. I did not.

Senator SMITH. Did you see the first lifeboat lowered?

Mr. ISMAY. That I could not answer, sir. I saw the first lifeboat lowered on the starboard side. What was going on on the port side I have no knowledge of.

Senator SMITH. It has been intimated, Mr. Ismay, that the first lifeboat did not contain the necessary number of men to man it.

Mr. ISMAY. As to that I have no knowledge, sir.

Senator SMITH. And that women were obliged to row the boat.

Mr. HUGHES: That is the second lifeboat, Senator.

Senator SMITH. The second lifeboat; and that women were obliged to row that boat from 10:30 o'clock at night until 7:30 o'clock the next morning.

Mr. ISMAY. The accident did not take place until 11 -

Senator SMITH. Well, from after 11:30 o'clock at night until between 6 and 7 o'clock the next morning.

Mr. ISMAY. Of that I have no knowledge.

Senator SMITH. Until the Carpathia overtook them. You have no knowledge of that?

Mr. ISMAY. Absolutely none, sir.

Senator SMITH. So far as your observation went, would you say that was not so?

Mr. ISMAY. I would not say either yes or no; but I did not see it.

Senator SMITH. When you first went on to the deck, you were only partially clothed?

Mr. ISMAY. That is all, sir.

Senator SMITH. And, as I understand, you went as far as to encounter an officer or steward?

Mr. ISMAY. Yes, sir.

Senator SMITH. And then returned?

Mr. ISMAY. That is right.

Senator SMITH. How long were you on the ship after the collision occurred?

Mr. ISMAY. That is a very difficult question to answer, sir. Practically until the time - almost until she sank.

Senator SMITH. How long did it take to lower and load a lifeboat?

Mr. ISMAY. I could not answer that.

Senator SMITH. Can you approximate it?

Mr. ISMAY. It is not possible for me to judge the time. I could not answer that.

Senator SMITH. Were you on the Titanic an hour after the collision?

Mr. ISMAY. Oh, yes.

Senator SMITH. How much longer?

Mr. ISMAY. I should think it was an hour and a quarter.

Senator SMITH. An hour and a quarter?

Mr. ISMAY. I should think that was it; perhaps longer.

Senator SMITH. Did you, during this time, see any of the passengers that you knew?

Mr. ISMAY. I really do not remember; I saw a great many passengers, but I do not think I paid much very attention to who they were. I do not remember recognizing any of them.

Senator SMITH. Did you know Charles M. Hayes?

Mr. ISMAY. Yes, sir.

Senator SMITH. Did you know of the presence of other Americans and Canadians of prominence?

Mr. ISMAY. No, sir; I knew Mr. Hayes was on board the ship.

Senator SMITH. You knew he was on the ship?

Mr. ISMAY. Yes; I have known him for some years.

Senator SMITH. But you did not see him after the accident occurred?

Mr. ISMAY. I never saw him after the accident; no.

Senator SMITH. And he is unaccounted for?

Mr. ISMAY. Yes, sir.

Senator SMITH. He was not among the saved?

Mr. ISMAY. No, sir.

Senator SMITH. What were the circumstances, Mr. Ismay, of your departure from the ship?

Mr. ISMAY. In what way?

Senator SMITH. Did the last boat that you went on leave the ship from some point near where you were?

Mr. ISMAY. I was immediately opposite the lifeboat when she left.

Senator SMITH. Immediately opposite?

Mr. ISMAY. Yes.

Senator SMITH. What were the circumstances of your departure from the ship? I ask merely that -

Mr. ISMAY. The boat was there. There was a certain number of men in the boat, and the officer called out asking if there were any more women, and there was no response, and there were no passengers left on the deck.

Senator SMITH. There were no passengers on the deck?

Mr. ISMAY. No, sir; and as the boat was in the act of being lowered away, I got into it.

Senator SMITH. At that time the Titanic was sinking?

Mr. ISMAY. She was sinking.

Senator SMITH. Where did this ship collide? Was it a side blow?

Mr. ISMAY. I have no knowledge, myself. I can only state what I have been told, that she hit the iceberg somewhere between the breakwater and the bridge.

Senator SMITH. State that again.

Mr. ISMAY. Between the breakwater and the bridge.

Senator SMITH. On the starboard side?

Mr. ISMAY. Yes.

Senator SMITH. Did you see any of the men passengers on that ship with life preservers on?

Mr. ISMAY. Nearly all passengers had life preservers on.

Senator SMITH. All that you saw?

Mr. ISMAY. All that I saw had life preservers on.

Senator SMITH. All of them that you saw?

Mr. ISMAY. Yes; as far as I can remember.

Senator SMITH. Naturally, you would remember that if you saw it? When you entered the lifeboat yourself, you say there were no passengers on that part of the ship?

Mr. ISMAY. None.

Senator SMITH. Did you, at any time, see any struggle among the men to get into these boats?

Mr. ISMAY. No.

Senator SMITH. Was there any attempt, as this boat was being lowered past the other decks, to have you take on more passengers?

Mr. ISMAY. None, sir. There were no passengers there to take on.

Senator SMITH. Before you boarded the lifeboat, did you see any of the passengers jump into the sea?

Mr. ISMAY. I did not.

Senator SMITH. After you had taken the lifeboat did you see any of the passengers or crew with life-saving apparatus on them in the sea?

Mr. ISMAY. No, sir.

Senator SMITH. What course was taken by the lifeboat in which you were after leaving the ship?

Mr. ISMAY. We saw a light some distance off to which we attempted to pull and which we thought was a ship.

Senator SMITH. Can you give the direction of it?

Mr. ISMAY. I could not give that.

Senator SMITH. But you saw a light?

Mr. ISMAY. Yes, sir.

Senator SMITH. And you attempted to pull this boat toward it?

Mr. ISMAY. Yes, sir.

Senator SMITH. How long were you in the open sea in this lifeboat?

Mr. ISMAY. I should think about four hours.

Senator SMITH.   Were there any other lifeboats in that vicinity?

Mr. ISMAY. Yes.

Senator SMITH. How many?

Mr. ISMAY. That I could not answer. I know there was one, because we hailed her. She had a light, and we hailed her, but got no answer from her.

Senator SMITH. You got no answer?

Mr. ISMAY. No, sir.

Senator SMITH. Did you see any rafts in the open sea?

Mr. ISMAY. No, sir; none.

Senator SMITH. Were there any other rafts on the Titanic that could have been utilized?

Mr. ISMAY. I believe not.

Senator SMITH. Were all of the lifeboats of one type?

Mr. ISMAY. No; there were four that are called collapsible boats.

Senator SMITH. What were the others?

Mr. ISMAY. Ordinary wooden boats.

Senator SMITH. How many were there?

Mr. ISMAY. I think there were 20 altogether.

Senator SMITH. Including both designs?

Mr. ISMAY.   Yes. Sixteen wooden boats and four collapsible boats, I think. I am not absolutely certain.

Senator SMITH.   When you reached the Carpathia, was your lifeboat taken aboard the Carpathia?

Mr. ISMAY. That I do not know.

Senator SMITH. Did you see any other lifeboats taken aboard the Carpathia?

Mr. ISMAY. I did not.

Senator SMITH. What was the method of getting you aboard the Carpathia?

Mr. ISMAY. We simply walked up a Jacob's ladder.

Senator SMITH. What was the condition of the sea at that time?

Mr. ISMAY. There was a little ripple on it, nothing more.

Senator SMITH. Do you know whether all the lifeboats that left the Titanic were accounted for?

Mr. ISMAY. I believe so. I do not know that of my own knowledge.

Senator SMITH. I think it has been suggested that two of them were engulfed.

Mr. ISMAY. Of that I know nothing.

Senator SMITH. You would know if that were true, would you not?

Mr. ISMAY. I have had no consultation with anybody since the accident with the exception of one officer.

Senator SMITH. Who was that?

Mr. ISMAY. Mr. Lightoller. I have spoken to no member of the crew or anybody since in regard to the accident.

Senator SMITH. What was Mr. Lightoller's position?

Mr. ISMAY. He was the second officer of the Titanic.

Senator SMITH. How many officers of the ship's crew were saved?

Mr. ISMAY. I am told four.

Senator SMITH. Can you give their names?

Mr. ISMAY. I can not.

Senator SMITH. Or their occupation?

Mr. ISMAY. I could not. The only one I know is Mr. Lightoller, who was the second officer.

Senator SMITH. I understand they are here.

Mr. ISMAY. I believe so; I do not know.

Senator SMITH. Mr. Ismay, what can you say about the sinking and disappearance of the ship? Can you describe the manner in which she went down?

Mr. ISMAY. I did not see her go down.

Senator SMITH. You did not see her go down?

Mr. ISMAY. No, sir.

Senator SMITH. How far were you from the ship?

Mr. ISMAY. I do not know how far we were away. I was sitting with my back to the ship. I was rowing all the time I was in the boat. We were pulling away.

Senator SMITH. You were rowing?

Mr. ISMAY. Yes; I did not wish to see her go down.

Senator SMITH. You did not care to see her go down?

Mr. ISMAY. No. I am glad I did not.

Senator SMITH. When you last saw her, were there indications that she had broken in two?

Mr. ISMAY. No, sir.

Senator SMITH. When did you last see her?

Mr. ISMAY. I really could not say. It might have been 10 minutes after we left her. It is impossible for me to give any judgment of the time. I could not do it.

Senator SMITH. Was there much apparent confusion on board when you saw her last?

Mr. ISMAY. I did not look to see, sir. My back was turned to her. I looked around once only, to see her red light - her green light, rather.

Senator SMITH. You never saw the captain again after you left him on the bridge?

Mr. ISMAY. No, sir.

Senator SMITH. Did you have any message from him?

Mr. ISMAY. Nothing.

Senator SMITH. Do you know how many wireless operators there were on board the ship?

Mr. ISMAY. I do not; but I presume there were two. There is always one on watch.

Senator SMITH. Do you know whether they survived?

Mr. ISMAY. I am told one of them did, but I do not know whether it is true or not. I really have not asked.

Senator SMITH. Were any of this crew enlisted men in the English Navy?

Mr., ISMAY: I do not know, sir. The ship's articles will show that.

Senator SMITH. Can you tell us anything about the inspection, and the certificate that was made and issued before sailing?

Mr. ISMAY. The ship receives a Board of Trade passenger certificate; otherwise she would not be allowed to carry passengers.

Senator SMITH. Do you know whether that was done?

Mr. ISMAY. You could not sail your ship without it; you could not get your clearance.

Senator SMITH. Do you know whether this ship was equipped with its full complement of lifeboats?

Mr. ISMAY. If she had not been, she could not have sailed. She would not have received her passenger certificate; therefore she must have been fully equipped.

Senator SMITH. Do you know whether these lifeboats were the lifeboats that were planned for the Titanic?

Mr. ISMAY. I do not quite understand what you mean, sir. I do not think lifeboats are ever built for the ship. Lifeboats are built to have a certain cubic capacity.

Senator SMITH. I understand that; but I mean whether these lifeboats were completed for the ship coincident with the completion of the ship, or whether the lifeboats, or any of them, were borrowed from the other ships of the White Star Line?

Mr. ISMAY. They certainly would not be borrowed from any other ship.

Senator SMITH. Do you recollect whether the lifeboat in which you left the ship was marked with the name Titanic on the boat or on the oars?

Mr. ISMAY. I have no idea. I presume oars would be marked. I do not know whether the boat was marked or not. She was a collapsible boat.

Senator SMITH. Can you recollect whether that was so?

Mr. ISMAY. I did not look to see whether the oars were marked. It would be a natural precaution to take?

Senator SMITH. Mr. Ismay, do you know about the boiler construction of the Titanic?

Mr. ISMAY. No, sir; I do not. May I suggest, gentlemen, if you wish any information in regard to the construction of the ship, in any manner, shape, or form, that I shall be only too pleased to arrange for one of the Harland & Wolff's people to come here and give you all the information you require; the plans and everything.

Senator SMITH. We are much obliged to you. There has been some suggestion by passengers who left the ship in lifeboats, that an explosion took place after this collision. Have you any knowledge on that point?

Mr. ISMAY. Absolutely none.

Senator SMITH. Do you think you would have known about that if it had occurred?

Mr. ISMAY. Yes; I should. Do you mean to say before the ship went down?

Senator SMITH. Yes.

Mr. ISMAY. Absolutely.

Senator SMITH. Mr. Ismay, do you know anything about the action of the amidship turbine; the number of revolutions?

Mr. ISMAY. No.

Mr. UHLER. The reciprocating engines, you say, were going at 75 or 72 revolutions at one time?

Mr. ISMAY. Yes.

Mr. UHLER. Have you any knowledge as to how many revolutions the amidship turbine was making?

Mr. ISMAY. No, sir. Those are all technical questions which can be answered by others, if you desire.

Senator NEWLANDS. What speed would 75 revolutions indicate?

Mr. ISMAY. I should think about 21 knots.

Senator NEWLANDS. What is that in miles?

Mr. ISMAY. It is in the ratio of 11 to 13; about 26 miles, I think.

Senator NEWLANDS. Mr. Ismay, did you have anything to do with the selection of the men who accompanied you in the last boat?

Mr. ISMAY. No, sir.

Senator NEWLANDS. How were they designated?

Mr. ISMAY. I presume by the officer who was in charge of the boat.

Senator NEWLANDS. Who was that?

Mr. ISMAY. Mr. Wilde.

Senator NEWLANDS. And he was what officer?

Mr. ISMAY. Chief officer.

Senator NEWLANDS. Was that done by lot or by selection?

Mr. ISMAY. I think these men were allotted certain posts.

Senator NEWLANDS. Indiscriminately?

Mr. ISMAY. No; I fancy at the time they had what they called, I think, the boat's crew list. That is all arranged beforehand.

Senator SMITH. Can you describe those rafts?

Mr. ISMAY. There were none on board the ship.

Senator SMITH. Did you see any rafts actually in service?

Mr. ISMAY. No, sir.

Senator SMITH. Is it customary for the White Star Line to carry rafts?

Mr. ISMAY. I believe in the olden days we carried rafts.

Senator SMITH. Recently that has not been done?

Mr. ISMAY. Not in the recent ships; no, sir.

Senator SMITH. Why?

Mr. ISMAY. I presume because they are not considered suitable.

Senator SMITH. Do you know what water capacity there was on that ship?

Mr. ISMAY. I do not, sir.

Senator SMITH. I mean, when she was stove in, how many compartments could be flooded with safety?

Mr. ISMAY. I beg your pardon, sir. I misunderstood your question. The ship was especially constructed to float with two compartments full of water.

Senator SMITH. She was constructed to float with two compartments full of water?

Mr. ISMAY. The ship was specially constructed so that she would float with any two compartments full of water. I think I am right in saying that there are very few ships - perhaps I had better not

say that, but I will continue, now that I have begun it - I believe there are very few ships to-day of which the same can be said.

When we built the Titanic we had that especially in mind. If this ship had hit the iceberg stem on, in all human probability she would have been here to-day.

Senator SMITH. If she had hit the iceberg head on, in all probability she would be here now?"

Mr. ISMAY. I say in all human probability that ship would have been afloat to-day.

Senator NEWLANDS. How did the ship strike the iceberg?

Mr. ISMAY. From information I have received, I think she struck the iceberg a glancing blow between the end of the forecastle and the captain's bridge, just aft of the foremast, sir.

Senator SMITH. I understood you to say a little while ago that you were rowing, with your back to the ship. If you were rowing and going away from the ship, you would naturally be facing the ship, would you not?

Mr. ISMAY. No; in these boats some row facing the bow of the boat and some facing the stern. I was seated with my back to the man who was steering, so that I was facing away from the ship.

Senator SMITH. You have stated that the ship was specially constructed so that she could float with two compartments filled with water?

Mr. ISMAY. Yes.

Senator SMITH. Is it your idea, then, that there were no two compartments left entire?

Mr. ISMAY. That I can not answer, sir. I am convinced that more than two compartments were filled. As I tried to explain to you last night, I think the ship's bilge was ripped open.

Senator NEWLANDS. The ship had 16 compartments?

Mr. ISMAY. I could not answer that, sir.

Senator NEWLANDS. Approximately?

Mr. ISMAY. Approximately. That information is absolutely at your disposal. Our shipbuilders will give it to you accurately.

Senator NEWLANDS. She was so built that if any two of these compartments should be filled with water she would still float?

Mr. ISMAY. Yes, sir; if any two of the largest compartments were filled with water she would still float.

Senator SMITH. Mr. Ismay, what time did you dine on Sunday evening?

Mr. ISMAY. At 7:30.

Senator SMITH. With whom?

Mr. ISMAY. With the doctor.

Senator SMITH. Did the captain dine with you?

Mr. ISMAY. He did not, sir.

Senator SMITH. When you went to the bridge after this collision, was there any ice on the decks?

Mr. ISMAY. I saw no ice at all, and no icebergs at all until daylight Monday morning.

Senator SMITH. Do you know whether any people were injured or killed from ice that came to the decks?

Mr. ISMAY. I do not, sir. I heard ice had been found on the decks, but it is only hearsay.

Senator SMITH. I think I asked you, but in case it appears that I have not, I will ask you again: Were all of the women and children saved?

Mr. ISMAY. I am afraid not, sir.

Senator SMITH. What proportion were saved?

Mr. ISMAY. I have no idea. I have not asked. Since the accident I have made very few inquiries of any sort.

Senator SMITH. Did any of the collapsible boats sink, to your knowledge, after leaving the ship?

Mr. ISMAY. No, sir.

Senator NEWLANDS. What was the full equipment of lifeboats for a ship of this size?

Mr. ISMAY. I could not tell you that, sir. That is covered by the Board of Trade regulations. She may have exceeded the Board of Trade regulations, for all I know. I could not answer that question. Anyhow, she had sufficient boats to obtain her passenger certificate, and therefore she must have been fully boated, according to the requirements of the English Board of Trade, which I understand are accepted by this country. Is not that so, General?

Mr. UHLER. Yes.

Senator SMITH. Mr. Ismay, did you in any manner attempt to influence or interfere with the wireless communication between the Carpathia and other stations?

Mr. ISMAY. No, sir. I think the captain of the Carpathia is here, and he will probably tell you that I was never out of my room from the time I got on board the Carpathia until the ship docked here last night. I never moved out of the room.

Senator SMITH. How were you dressed? Were you completely dressed when you went into the lifeboat?

Mr. ISMAY. I had a suit of pajamas on, a pair of slippers, a suit of clothes, and an overcoat.

Senator SMITH. How many men, officers and crew, were there on this boat?

Mr. ISMAY. There were no officers.

Senator SMITH. I mean the officers of the ship.

Mr. ISMAY. How many officers were there on the ship?

Senator SMITH. Yes, and how many in the crew?

Mr. ISMAY. I think there were seven officers on the ship.

Senator SMITH. And how many in the crew?

Mr. ISMAY. I do not know the full number of the crew. There were seven officers - or nine officers; there are always three officers on watch.

Senator SMITH. And how many men were in the lifeboat with you?

Mr. ISMAY. Oh, I could not tell. I suppose nine or ten.

Senator SMITH. Do you know who they were?

Mr. ISMAY. I do not. Mr. [William] Carter, a passenger, was one. I do not know who the others were; third-class passengers, I think. In fact, all the people on the boat, as far as I could see, were third-class passengers.

Senator SMITH. Did they all survive, and were they all taken aboard the Carpathia?

Mr. ISMAY. They all survived, yes.

Senator SMITH. You have indicated your willingness to supply the committee with any data or information that may be necessary regarding the construction and equipment of this vessel?

Mr. ISMAY. Any information or any data the committee may wish is absolutely at their disposal.

Senator SMITH. And you have indicated your willingness to meet our full committee?

Mr. ISMAY. At any time you wish, sir.

Senator SMITH. And I suppose this includes the surviving officers?

Mr. ISMAY. Certainly, sir. Anybody that you wish is absolutely at your disposal.

Senator SMITH. What are your own immediate plans?

Mr. ISMAY. I understand that depends on you.

Senator SMITH. I thank you, in behalf of my associates and myself, for responding so readily this morning, and for your statements; and I am going to ask you to hold yourself subject to our wishes during the balance of the day.

For the Convenience of the Captain of the Carpathia I am going to call him at this time.

Mr. ISMAY. I am entirely at your disposal at any time, sir.

Senator SMITH. The committee has decided to call the captain of the Carpathia as the next witness.

TESTIMONY OF CAPT. ARTHUR HENRY ROSTRON.

Captain, SS Carpathia

The Witness was sworn by the chairman.

Senator SMITH. Please give your full name and address.

Mr. ROSTRON. Arthur Henry Rostron, Woodville, Victoria Road, Crosby, Liverpool.

Senator SMITH. What is your business, Captain?

Mr. ROSTRON. Seaman.

Senator SMITH. How long have you been engaged in this business?

Mr. ROSTRON. Twenty-seven years.

Senator SMITH. What positions have you filled?

Mr. ROSTRON. Every rank in the merchant service up to captain.

Senator SMITH. In what companies or on what lines?

Mr. ROSTRON. First of all I was two years as a cadet on the training ship Conway in the Mersey, Liverpool, after which I went under sail as an apprentice with Williams & Milligan's ships. I was an apprentice for three years, after which I was second mate, after passing my examinations. Then, after getting my mates certificate, I went as mate on another sailing ship. Then I passed for extra master and joined the Cunard Steamship Co. in 1895.

Senator SMITH. You are now captain of the Carpathia?

Mr. ROSTRON. I am now captain of the Carpathia, Cunard Line.

Senator SMITH. How long have you been captain of the Carpathia?

Mr. ROSTRON. My appointment on the Carpathia dates from the 18th of January.

Senator SMITH. Of this year?

Mr. ROSTRON. Of this year; yes sir.

Senator SMITH. Were you captain of any other vessel?

Mr. ROSTRON. The whole of last year, from the 1st of January of last year, I was captain of the Penonia.

Senator SMITH. Of the same line?

Mr. ROSTRON. Of the same line. Previous to that I was captain of several other smaller cargo boats running between Liverpool and the Mediterranean.

Senator SMITH. What day did you sail with the Carpathia from New York last?

Mr. ROSTRON. The 11th of April.

Senator SMITH. And where were you headed?

Mr. ROSTRON. We were bound for Liverpool, Genoa, Naples, Trieste, and Fiume.

Senator SMITH. How many passengers did you have on board the Carpathia when you sailed from New York?

Mr. ROSTRON. That I am not prepared to answer, sir. I can not give you the exact number.

Senator SMITH. About how many?

Mr. ROSTRON. One hundred and fifty first; 50 second; and about 560 or 575, third. That is approximately.

Senator SMITH. Your first stop would have been Gibraltar?

Mr. ROSTRON. Gibraltar; yes sir.

Senator SMITH. What time in the day did you leave New York?

Mr. ROSTRON. At noon on Thursday.

Senator SMITH. I wish you would tell the committee what occurred after that day, as nearly as you can, up to the present time.

Mr. ROSTRON. We backed out from the dock at noon on Thursday. We proceeded down the river, the weather being fine and clear, and we left the pilot at the pilot boat and passed the Ambrose Channel Lightship about 2 o'clock p.m. I can not give you the exact time, now, because, as a matter of fact, I have not looked at a single date or time of any kind. I have not had the time to do so.

Senator SMITH. I mean approximately?

Mr. ROSTRON. From that up to Sunday midnight we had fine, clear weather, and everything was going on without any trouble of any kind.

At 12:35 a. m. on Monday I was informed of the urgent distress signal from the Titanic.

Senator SMITH. By whom?

Mr. ROSTRON. By our wireless operator, and also by the first officer.

The wireless operator had taken the message and run with it up to the bridge, and gave it to the first officer who was in charge, with a junior officer with him, and both ran down the ladder to my door and called me. I had only just turned in. It was an urgent distress signal from the Titanic, requiring immediate assistance and giving me his position.

The position of the Titanic at the time was 41□ 46" north, 50□ 14" west. I can not give you our correct position, but we were then -

Senator SMITH. Did you give the hour?

Mr. ROSTRON. Yes, 12:35; that was our apparent time. I can give you the New York time, if you would rather have it?

Senator SMITH. Yes; please do so.

Mr. ROSTRON. The New York time at 12:35 was 10:45 p. m. Sunday night.

Immediately on getting the message, I gave the order to turn the ship around, and immediately I had given that order I asked the operator if he was absolutely sure it was a distress signal from the Titanic. I asked him twice.

Senator SMITH. Just what was that signal?

Mr. ROSTRON. I did not ask him. He simply told me that he had received a distress signal from the Titanic, requiring immediate assistance, and gave me his position; and he assured me he was absolutely certain of the message.

In the meantime I was dressing, and I picked up our position on my chart, and set a course to pick up the Titanic. The course was north 52 degrees west true 58 miles from my position.

I then sent for the chief engineer. In the meantime I was dressing and seeing the ship put on her course. The chief engineer came up. I told him to call another watch of stokers and make all possible speed to the Titanic, as she was in trouble.

He ran down immediately and told me my orders would be carried out at once.

After that I gave the first officer, who was in charge of the bridge, orders to knock off all work which the men were doing on deck, the watch on deck, and prepare all our lifeboats, take out the spare gear, and have them all ready for turning outboard.

Immediately I had done that I sent for the heads of the different departments, the English doctor, the purser, and the chief steward, and they came to my cabin, and then I issued my orders. I do not know whether you care to hear what my orders were exactly.

Senator SMITH. Yes, sir; we would like to hear them.

Mr. ROSTRON. As a matter of fact, I have them all written down here. We carry an English doctor, an Italian doctor, and a Hungarian doctor. My orders were these:

English doctor, with assistants, to remain in first-class dining room.

Italian doctor, with assistants, to remain in second-class dining room.

Hungarian doctor, with assistants, to remain in third-class dining room.

Each doctor to have supplies of restoratives, stimulants, and everything to hand for immediate needs of probable wounded or sick.

Purser, with assistant purser and chief steward, to receive the passengers, etc., at different gangways, controlling our own stewards in assisting Titanic passengers to the dining rooms, etc.; also to get Christian and surnames of all survivors as soon as possible to send by wireless.

Inspector, steerage stewards, and master at arms to control our own steerage passengers and keep them out of the third-class dining hall, and also to keep them out of the way and off the deck to prevent confusion.

Chief steward: That all hands would be called and to have coffee, etc., ready to serve out to all our crew.

Have coffee, tea, soup, etc., in each saloon, blankets in saloons, at the gangways, and some for the boats.

To see all rescued cared for and immediate wants attended to.

My cabin and all officials' cabins to be given up. Smoke rooms, library, etc., dining rooms, would be utilized to accommodate the survivors.

All spare berths in steerage to be utilized for Titanic's passengers, and get all our own steerage passengers grouped together.

Stewards to be placed in each alleyway to reassure our own passengers, should they inquire about noise in getting our boats out, etc., or the working of engines.

To all I strictly enjoined the necessity for order, discipline and quietness and to avoid all confusion.

Chief and first officers: All the hands to be called; get coffee, etc. Prepare and swing out all boats.

All gangway doors to be opened.

Electric sprays in each gangway and over side.

A block with line rove hooked in each gangway.

A chair sling at each gangway, for getting up sick or wounded.

Boatswains' chairs. Pilot ladders and canvas ash bags to be at each gangway, the canvas ash bags for children.

I may state the canvas ash bags were of great assistance in getting the infants and children aboard.

Cargo falls with both ends clear; bowlines in the ends, and bights secured along ship's sides, for boat ropes or to help the people up.

Heaving lines distributed along the ship's side, and gaskets handy near gangways for lashing people in chairs, etc.

Forward derricks, topped and rigged, and steam on winches; also told off officers for different stations and for certain eventualities.

Ordered company's rockets to be fired at 2:45 a. m. and every quarter of an hour after to reassure Titanic.

This is a copy of what I am sending to our own company.

Senator SMITH. We would like to have you leave a copy of that with the committee, if you can.

Mr. ROSTRON. Yes, sir; I shall do it with pleasure.

One more thing:

As each official saw everything in readiness, he reported to me personally on the bridge that all my orders were carried out, enumerating the same, and that everything was in readiness.

This was at 3:45. That was a quarter of an hour before we got up to the scene of the disaster. The details of all this work I left to the several officials, and I am glad to say that they were most efficiently carried out.

Senator SMITH. I should judge from what you say that you made 19 1/4 knots from the time you got the signal of distress from the Titanic, until you reached the scene of the wreck or loss?

Mr. ROSTRON. No, it was 58 miles, and it took us three and a half hours.

Mr. UHLER. From 12:35 to 3:45?

Mr. ROSTRON. No; 3:45 is when they reported to me. I have not got to the time of arrival at the scene of action yet. I stopped my engines at 4 o'clock, and I was then close to the first boat.

Senator SMITH. Just proceed, in your own way.

Mr. ROSTRON. After interviewing the heads of the departments, I went on the bridge and remained there. While I was up there I made inquiries making sure that my orders were all being carried out, and that everything possible was being done.

At 2:40, I saw a flare, about half a point on the port bow, and immediately took it for granted that it was the Titanic itself, and I remarked that she must be still afloat, as I knew we were a long way off, and it seemed so high.

However, soon after seeing the flare I made out an iceberg about a point on the port bow, to which I had to port to keep well clear of. Knowing that the Titanic had struck ice, of course I had to take extra care and every precaution to keep clear of anything that might look like ice.

Between 2:45 and 4 o'clock, the time I stopped my engines, we were passing icebergs on every side and making them ahead and having to alter our course several times to clear the bergs.

At 4 o'clock I stopped.

At 4:10 I got the first boat alongside.

Previous to getting the first boat alongside, however, I saw an iceberg close to me, right ahead, and I had to starboard to get out of the way. And I picked him up on the weather side of the ship. I had to clear this ice.

I am on the scene of action now. This is 4:10 with the first boat alongside.

Senator SMITH. You are picking up these people now?

Mr. ROSTRON. Yes.

Senator SMITH. Please describe that in your own way.

Mr. ROSTRON. We picked up the first boat, and the boat was in charge of an officer. I saw that he was not under full control

40

of this boat, and the officer sung out to me that he only had one seaman in the boat, so I had to maneuver the ship to get as close to the boat as possible, as I knew well it would be difficult to do the pulling. However, they got alongside, and they got them up all right.

By the time we had the first boat's people it was breaking day, and then I could see the remaining boats all around within an area of about 4 miles. I also saw icebergs all around me. There were about 20 icebergs that would be anywhere from about 150 to 200 feet high and numerous smaller bergs; also numerous what we call "growlers." You would not call them bergs. They were anywhere from 10 to 12 feet high and 10 to 15 feet long above the water.

I maneuvered the ship and we gradually got all the boats together. We got all the boats alongside and all the people up aboard by 8:30.

I was then very close to where the Titanic must have gone down, as there was a lot of hardly wreckage but small pieces of broken-up stuff nothing in the way of anything large.

At 8 o'clock the Leyland Line steamer Californian hove up, and we exchanged messages. I gave them the notes by semaphore about the Titanic going down, and that I had got all the passengers from the boats; but we were then not quite sure whether we could account for all the boats. I told them: "Think one boat still unaccounted for." He then asked me if he should search around, and I said, "Yes, please." It was then 10:50.

I want to go back again, a little bit.

At 8:30 all the people were on board. I asked for the purser, and told him that I wanted to hold a service, a short prayer of thankfulness for those rescued and a short burial service for those who were lost. I consulted with Mr. Ismay. I ran down for a moment and told them that I wished to do this, and Mr. Ismay left everything in my hands.

I then got an Episcopal clergyman, one of our passengers, and asked him if he would do this for me, which he did, willingly.

While they were holding the service, I was on the bridge, of course, and I maneuvered around the scene of the wreckage. We saw nothing except one body.

Senator SMITH. Floating?

Mr. ROSTRON. Floating, sir.

Senator SMITH. With a life preserver on?

Mr. ROSTRON. With a life preserver on. That is the only body I saw.

Senator SMITH. Was it male or female?

Mr. ROSTRON. Male. It appeared to me to be one of the crew. He was only about 100 yards from the ship. We could see him quite distinctly, and saw that he was absolutely dead. He was lying on his side like this [indicating] and his head was awash. Of course he could not possibly have been alive and remain in that position. I did not take him aboard. For one reason, the Titanic's passengers then were

knocking about the deck and I did not want to cause any unnecessary excitement or any more hysteria among them, so I steamed past, trying to get them not to see it.

From the boats we took three dead men, who had died of exposure.

Senator SMITH. From the lifeboats?

Mr. ROSTRON. From the lifeboats; yes, sir.

Senator SMITH. Do you know from which boats they were taken?

42

Mr. ROSTRON. No, sir; I am only giving you the general news now. We took three dead men from the boats, and they were brought on board. Another man was brought up - I think he was one of the crew - who died that morning about 10 o'clock, I think, and he, with the other three, were buried at 4 o'clock in the afternoon.

Senator SMITH. At sea?

Mr. ROSTRON. At sea.

Senator SMITH. Did they have anything on their persons by which they could be identified?

Mr. ROSTRON. One of my own officers and the Titanic's officers identified the bodies, as far as possible, and took everything from them that could be of the slightest clue or use. Nothing was left but their clothes. There was very little taken, of course. But, as regards details, I can not give you much. I have been too busy.

Senator SMITH. You have not the names of these men?

Mr. ROSTRON. We have the names.

Senator SMITH. You have not them here with you?

Mr. ROSTRON. I have not got them with me; no, sir.

Senator SMITH. Were they men or women?

Mr. ROSTRON. Men. There were several ladies in the boats. They were slightly injured about the arms and things of that kind, of course; although I must say, from the very start, all these people behaved magnificently. As each boat came alongside everyone was calm, and they kept perfectly still in their boats. They were quiet and orderly, and each person came up the ladder, or was pulled up, in turn as they were told off. There was no confusion whatever among the passengers. They behaved magnificently - every one of them.

As they came aboard, they were, of course, attended to. My instructions had already been given to that effect.

Senator SMITH. Captain, how many lifeboats were there?

Mr. ROSTRON. We had 15 lifeboats alongside with passengers in them.

Senator SMITH. Of both types?

Mr. ROSTRON. Wait a moment, please.

There were 15 lifeboats alongside. We accounted for those with passengers in them. There was one lifeboat that we saw that was close to the ship, but it had been abandoned because it had got damaged, and was in a sinking condition. The officer had taken all the people out of that lifeboat, and left it absolutely vacant. There was no one in it. It was empty.

Senator SMITH. What type of boat was it?

Mr. ROSTRON. That was a lifeboat. It had been damaged. We had two berthen boats.

Senator SMITH. Collapsible boats?

Mr. ROSTRON. Hardly collapsible; it is a flat raft boat, with collapsible canvas sides, about two feet deep.

Senator SMITH. To hold how many people?

Mr. ROSTRON. One of those boats would hold 60 to 75 comfortably.

Senator SMITH. How many of those were there?

Mr. ROSTRON. We accounted for two. One of these berthen boats capsized. That was three.

Senator SMITH. As these boats were emptied, and the occupants taken aboard the Carpathia what was done with the boats?

Mr. ROSTRON. The boats were kept alongside.

44

Senator SMITH. Just in what shape were they left afloat, or were they in some way taken on the decks?

Mr. ROSTRON. Yes, sir; I am going to tell you that now. As the people came out, we left the boats alongside. Of course lots of gear had been knocked out of the boats and thrown out of the way of the people as they were getting up; so, while they were holding this service and while I was cruising around, I had had all of my boats swung out, ready for lowering over, and while they were getting all the people aboard from the boats, I got the spare men and some of my officers, and swung my boats inboard again, and landed them on their blocks and secured them, and swung the davits out again, disconnected the falls again, and got up the Titanic's boats. While I was cruising around, I was also getting these boats up. I got seven of the Titanic's boats up in our davits, and six up on the forecastle head with the forward derricks; so that is 13 boats in all.

Senator SMITH. What did you do with these boats?

Mr. ROSTRON. We pulled them up the davits.

Senator SMITH. Did you bring them into port?

Mr. ROSTRON. Yes; and last night, previous to coming into the dock, we got some tenders off and lowered all the boats in the water, and these tenders took them away. Where they took them I do not know. But we had these boats still left on the forecastle head, and they would have been put into the dock during the day.

Senator SMITH. Have you examined those boats personally?

Mr. ROSTRON. I have only been in one or two of them; looked at them.

Senator SMITH. Can you tell from what you saw of them whether they were marked Titanic?

Mr. ROSTRON. They were all marked "Titanic," as they came up.

Senator SMITH. Were they apparently new boats?

Mr. ROSTRON. They were all brand new.

Senator SMITH. They were all brand new?

Mr. ROSTRON. Yes; as far as I could see. They appeared to me to be absolutely new boats.

Senator SMITH. All conforming to the regulations of the British Board of Trade?

Mr. ROSTRON. Absolutely.

Senator SMITH. And as good as you would have had if you were to specify them yourself?

Mr. ROSTRON. Quite.

Senator SMITH. Did you see any bodies afloat, except as you have described?

Mr. ROSTRON. Only one; no more - no others.

Senator SMITH. Did you have any information as to whether the passengers or crew of the Titanic had made use of their life preservers?

Mr. ROSTRON. I had very little opportunity of being amongst the passengers or any of them.

To tell you the truth, I have been on the bridge, or about my duties most of the time. I had, however, one or two conversations with the passengers on Tuesday afternoon. That was the only time I had anything to do with the people, as I heard then that all the people on the Titanic, as far as they could see, had life belts on. They had all been supplied with life belts.

Senator SMITH. I assume that you kept watch to see whether there was any of these people afloat?

Mr. ROSTRON.   Precisely. I was cruising all around the vicinity of the disaster.

Senator SMITH.   How long did you cruise around there?

Mr. ROSTRON.   In the actual vicinity of the disaster?

Senator SMITH.   Yes.

Mr. ROSTRON.   Half an hour.

Senator SMITH.   During that time was there a swirl or any unnatural condition of the sea?

Mr. ROSTRON.   Nothing whatever. The wind and sea were then beginning to get up. There was a moderate breeze blowing then, and a little slop of the sea.

Senator SMITH.   Have you any idea how much depth of water there was about that point?

Mr. ROSTRON.   Yes; about two thousand and odd fathoms.

Senator SMITH.   Two thousand and odd fathoms?

Mr. ROSTRON.   Yes; I looked on the chart.

Senator SMITH.   Have you concluded that you did not see the ill-fated ship at all?

Mr. ROSTRON.   Oh, no; we arrived an hour and a half after she went down; after the last of her was seen.

Senator SMITH.   What was the last message you had from the ship?

Mr. ROSTRON.   "Engine room nearly full."

Senator SMITH.   "Engine room nearly full"?

Mr. ROSTRON.   Yes.

Senator SMITH.   At what hour was that?

Mr. ROSTRON.   That would have been about 1 o'clock. That would be 25 minutes after.

Senator SMITH.   Was that all?

Mr. ROSTRON. That was the last message we got. It was either "Engine room nearly full," or "Engine room full," or "Engine room filling." The exact words I could not give you. The impression was quite enough for me, as to the condition the ship was in.

Senator SMITH. And you then told them how near you were?

Mr. ROSTRON. Yes. From the very first I sent a message to the Titanic - telling them, "Coming immediately to your assistance. Expect to arrive half past 4-" No; it was, "Expect to arrive in four hours," because I had not then got up full speed.

Senator SMITH. Did you personally know the captain of the Titanic?

Mr. ROSTRON. I knew him; yes.

Senator SMITH. How long had you known him?

Mr. ROSTRON. I had met him 15 years ago. I have only met him about three times altogether.

Senator SMITH. In your company, who is the master of a ship at sea?

Mr. ROSTRON. The captain.

Senator SMITH. In absolute control?

Mr. ROSTRON. In absolute control, legal and otherwise. No one can interfere.

Senator SMITH. I suppose if this had not been so, you would not have felt it proper to have gone off your course quite so far?

Mr. ROSTRON. Quite so.

Senator SMITH. Are there prescribed routes at sea that are so definite in their character as to be well understood by mariners?

Mr. ROSTRON.   They are. I may state this: That the position given me by the Titanic was absolutely correct and she was absolutely on her track, bound for New York.

Senator SMITH.   What would you call that course, Captain, that the Titanic was taking for New York, as to whether it would be northerly or southerly?

Mr. ROSTRON.   Oh, she was then - I forget the true course now, but she had passed what we call the corner on the great circle. It is some years since I was in the North Atlantic trade. I have been in the Mediterranean trade, and I have forgotten.

Mr. UHLER.   He is not speaking of your compass course.

Mr. ROSTRON.   I am giving the true course.

Mr. UHLER.   He is asking whether the Titanic was on the northerly course or the southerly route?

Mr. ROSTRON.   Oh. He was on the southerly route.

Senator SMITH.   What do you mean by that?

Mr. ROSTRON.   He makes a great circle on the most southerly route, to avoid all ice, as nearly as possible. That is 42 north and 47 west. That is what we call the first corner. That is the great circle track from Queenstown down to the corner. From there he takes a straight course - I forget, now, the actual course.

Senator SMITH.   Do you regard the route he was taking as entirely practical and appropriate at this time of the year?

Mr. ROSTRON.   Quite so. This is most exceptional.

Senator SMITH.   Having the warning that icebergs were in that vicinity, could he, under those circumstances have changed his course somewhat to avoid them?

Mr. ROSTRON.   That is impossible for me to tell. All I know is that he was on the track of the western bound steamers, on his proper track, where he ought to have been.

Senator SMITH. At this time of year?

Mr. ROSTRON. At this time of year.

Senator SMITH. Is not that the shortest route from Liverpool to New York?

Mr. ROSTRON. No; it is the longest.

Senator SMITH. The longest?

Mr. ROSTRON. Yes, sir.

Senator SMITH. What would have been the shortest?

Mr. ROSTRON. The shortest route is after August, if I remember right; from September to January. From September to January, I think, is the shortest route.

Senator SMITH. But what would that be?

Mr. ROSTRON. Oh, well; up north.

Senator SMITH. How far north?

Mr. ROSTRON. It would be probably a couple of hundred miles north.

Senator SMITH. Would you regard the course taken by the Titanic in this trial trip as appropriate and safe and wise at this time of the year?

Mr. ROSTRON. Quite so.

Senator SMITH. What would be a safe, reasonable speed for a vessel of that size on such a course and in proximity of icebergs?

Mr. ROSTRON. Of course I do not know the ship. I know absolutely nothing about her.

Senator SMITH. How would you have felt yourself about it. Suppose you had been taking that course with your ship; how fast would you have felt it prudent to go in such a situation?

Mr. ROSTRON. I can only tell you this, gentlemen, I knew there was ice about.

50

Senator SMITH. How did you know it?

Mr. ROSTRON. From the Titanic.

Senator SMITH. From the Titanic's message?

Mr. ROSTRON. Precisely. He told me he had struck ice.

Senator SMITH. Did you know it any other way?

Mr. ROSTRON. No, sir; that was the first intimation I had that there was ice there.

Senator SMITH. You did not know it until you saw it yourself?

Mr. ROSTRON. I knew the Titanic had struck ice. Therefore, I was prepared to be in the vicinity of ice when I was getting near him, because if he had struck a berg and I was going to his position I knew very well that there must be ice about. I went full speed, all we could -

Senator SMITH. You went full speed?

Mr. ROSTRON. I did, and doubled my lookouts, and took extra precautions and exerted extra vigilance. Every possible care was taken. We were all on the qui vive.

Senator SMITH. You had a smaller ship, however, and it would respond more readily to a signal?

Mr. ROSTRON. No.

Senator SMITH. Would it not?

Mr. ROSTRON. No, sir; it would not. I do not maintain that, for one moment.

Senator SMITH. How many men were on the bridge, on the lookout, so to speak, in that situation, on your ship?

Mr. ROSTRON. There were three officers with me: A quartermaster, one man in the crow's nest, and two men in the eyes of the ship - that is, right forward on the deck, nearer to the water than the crow's nest.

Senator SMITH. Was that the ordinary complement, or did you put them there because of that danger?

Mr. ROSTRON. I put an extra lookout on forward.

Senator SMITH. An extra lookout?

Mr. ROSTRON. Yes; and the officer came up extra with me. I had another officer up with me, extra. He came up voluntarily.

Senator SMITH. What would be the ordinary complement?

Mr. ROSTRON. The ordinary complement of a night lookout, two men. We keep one in the crow's nest and one in the eyes - that is, right forward.

Senator SMITH. Was there any special suffering of the Titanic's passengers after they got aboard the Carpathia?

Mr. ROSTRON. I never heard of anything special. I can not give you any medical reports, as I have not received them yet. All I know is that the second day, Tuesday morning, the doctor came to me and said he was pleased to say that there was any entirely clean bill of health.

Senator SMITH. No damage, so far as you know, was done by one to the other, and there was no trouble or difficulty?

Mr. ROSTRON. No, no; none whatever. I never heard of anything of that kind, never.

Senator SMITH. How many lifeboats do you carry on the Carpathia?

Mr. ROSTRON. We carry 20.

Senator SMITH. What is their capacity?

Mr. ROSTRON. I am not prepared to say at the present moment. I can not say; I really forget.

Senator SMITH. Do you carry 20 in obedience to certain regulations of the British Board of Trade?

Mr. ROSTRON. I think it is 20; yes.

Senator SMITH. What is your gross tonnage?

Mr. ROSTRON. Thirteen thousand six hundred tons.

Senator SMITH. That is the total capacity of your ship, the tonnage?

Mr. ROSTRON. Thirteen thousand six hundred.

Senator SMITH. What is it as to passengers?

Mr. ROSTRON. I can not tell you. I have not come here with any data. I have not looked up anything, and was absolutely unprepared for any questions. I have been too busy.

Senator SMITH. What did you say was the tonnage of your ship?

Mr. ROSTRON. Thirteen thousand six hundred tons.

Senator SMITH. What was the tonnage of the Titanic?

Mr. UHLER. It was 45,629 tons.

Senator SMITH. Are these regulations of the British Board of Trade new regulations or old regulations?

Mr. ROSTRON. They are of recent date.

Senator SMITH. The fact that, under these regulations, you are obliged to carry 20 lifeboats and the Titanic was only obliged to carry 20, with her additional tonnage, indicates either that these regulations were prescribed long ago -

Mr. ROSTRON. (interposing): No, sir; it has nothing to do with that. What it has to do with is the ship itself. The ships are built nowadays to be practically unsinkable, and each ship is supposed to be a lifeboat in itself. The boats are merely supposed to be put on as a standby. The ships are supposed to be built, and the naval architects say they are, unsinkable under certain conditions. What the exact conditions are, I do not know, as to whether it is with alternate compartments full, or what it may be. That is why in our ship we carry more lifeboats, for the simple reason that we are built differently from the Titanic; differently constructed.

Senator SMITH. Approximately how many passengers are provided for on the Carpathia? I do not ask you to be accurate about it, but approximately how many?

Mr. ROSTRON. How many did we approximately provide for on the voyage from New York?

Mr. UHLER. What is your British allowance?

Mr. ROSTRON. Two thousand two hundred third, and about 250 first and second combined.

Senator SMITH. That makes 2,450. Give us your crew complement.

Mr. ROSTRON. That, of course, varies. We have about 300 aboard now.

Senator SMITH. How many officers?

Mr. ROSTRON. Six officers.

Senator SMITH. You say the captain of a ship is vested ordinarily with absolute control and discretion over the movements of his vessel?

Mr. ROSTRON. Absolutely. I wish to qualify that, however. By law, the captain of the vessel has absolute control, but suppose we get orders from the owners of the vessel to do a certain thing and we do not carry it out. The only thing is then that we are liable to dismissal. I shall give you an illustration of what I mean by that, as regards receiving orders, and so on. When I turned back to New York, I sent my message to the Cunard Co. telling them that I was proceeding to New York unless otherwise ordered. You see what I mean there? I said, "For many considerations, consider New York most advisable."

Senator SMITH. And you immediately reversed your course?

Mr. ROSTRON. I came right around for New York immediately, and returned to New York. Would you like to know my reasons for coming back to New York?

Senator SMITH. Yes.

Mr. ROSTRON. The first and principal reason was that we had all these women aboard, and I knew they were hysterical and in a bad state. I knew very well, also, that you would want all the news possible. I knew very well, further, that if I went to Halifax, we could get them there all right, but I did not know how many of these people were half dead, how many were injured, or how many were really sick, or anything like that. I knew, also, that if we went to Halifax, we would have the possibility of coming across more ice, and I knew very well what the effect of that would be on people who had had the experience these people had had. I knew what that would be the whole time we were in the vicinity of ice. I took that into consideration. I knew very well that if we went to Halifax it would be a case of railway journey for these passengers, as I knew they would have to go to New York, and there would be all the miseries of that.

Furthermore, I did not know what the condition of the weather might be, or what accommodation I could give them in Halifax, and that was a great consideration - one of the greatest considerations that made me turn back.

Mr. UHLER. And the chances for fine weather were better coming to New York than going to Halifax?

Mr. ROSTRON. Yes, sir.

Senator SMITH. Your message to your company was practically notice that you had done this?

55

Mr. ROSTRON. I had done it; but the message did not get off until Monday evening.

Senator SMITH. You were then -

Mr. ROSTRON. (interrupting). When I sent that message we had been on our way 12 hours.

Senator SMITH. Captain, is it customary to take orders from a director or a general officer of the company aboard?

Mr. ROSTRON. No, sir.

Senator SMITH. From whom do you take orders?

Mr. ROSTRON. From no one.

Senator SMITH. Aboard ship?

Mr. ROSTRON. At sea, immediately I leave port until I arrive at port, the captain is in absolute control and takes orders from no one. I have never known it in our company or any other big company when a director or a managing owner would issue orders on that ship. It matters not who comes on board that ship they are either passengers or crew. There is no official status and no authority whatever with them.

Senator SMITH. You say, Captain, that you ran under a full head of steam?

Mr. ROSTRON. Yes.

Senator SMITH. Toward the Titanic?

Mr. ROSTRON. Yes, sir.

Senator SMITH. Would you have done so in the nighttime?

Mr. ROSTRON. It was in the nighttime. I can confess this much, that if I had known at the time there was so much ice about, I should not; but I was right in it then. I could see the ice.

I knew I was perfectly clear. There is one other consideration: Although I was running a risk with my own ship and my own passengers, I also had to consider what I was going for.

Senator SMITH. To save the lives of others?

Mr. ROSTRON. Yes; I had to consider the lives of others.

Senator SMITH. You were prompted by your interest in humanity?

Mr. ROSTRON. Absolutely.

Senator SMITH. And you took the chance?

Mr. ROSTRON. It was hardly a chance. Of course it was a chance, but at the same time I knew quite what I was doing. I considered that I was perfectly free, and that I was doing perfectly right in what I did.

Senator SMITH. I suppose no criticism has been passed upon you for it?

Mr. ROSTRON. No.

Senator SMITH. In fact, I think I may say, for my associates, that your conduct deserves the highest praise.

Mr. ROSTRON. I thank you, sir.

Senator SMITH. And we are very grateful to you, Captain, for coming here.

I understand it is your purpose to leave this afternoon?

Mr. ROSTRON. Yes; I think we sail at 4 o'clock.

Senator SMITH. If we should desire to get into communication again, what are your plans for the future? Are you headed for the south of Europe?

Mr. ROSTRON. We go to Gibraltar. I am just going by the same old route as before - Gibraltar, Genoa, Naples, Trieste, Fiume.

Mr. UHLER. Fifty days back to New York?

Mr. ROSTRON. A little less than that. About 43 days back. We sail about every seven weeks.

Senator SMITH. Did I ask you about the number of passengers that died aboard ship on your way to New York?

Mr. ROSTRON. No, sir. None died on the ship; so far as I am aware. We took three bodies from the boats, already dead, and the third man who died on board from exposure, who was taken on board from the lifeboat, was a seaman. I am almost sure of my statement that he was a seaman.

Senator SMITH. In the first lifeboat you say there was only one man?

Mr. ROSTRON. No; only one seaman. I think there were two more men. To tell the truth, I am not quite sure how many men there were.

Senator SMITH. Were there any officers?

Mr. ROSTRON. One officer.

Senator SMITH. One officer and one seaman?

Mr. ROSTRON. And one seaman, yes.

Senator SMITH. How many men?

Mr. ROSTRON. I can not tell you. I can not give you the number of any men or seamen in any of the boats, even approximately, now.

Senator SMITH. These lifeboats, of course, were being propelled by oats?

Mr. ROSTRON. Yes, sir.

Senator SMITH. Were there any women using these oars?

Mr. ROSTRON. There were.

Senator SMITH. In how many boats?

Mr. ROSTRON. I saw women, I think, in at least two boats rowing.

Senator SMITH. How many women using the oats?

58

Mr. ROSTRON. In one I saw two. It is very hard to give the exact number, because one or two of the boats were rather crowded, especially one boat that had got damaged and was foundering. That boat was very crowded. I could not say how many women were pulling. I saw certainly two or three women pulling at the oars. I know, as a matter of fact, in one boat there were two or three women pulling.

Senator SMITH. In what boat did Mr. Ismay come?

Mr. ROSTRON. I have not the faintest idea. The first I knew that Mr. Ismay was aboard was when we got the last boat alongside, and we were getting the last passengers aboard.

Senator SMITH. You do not remember the number of seamen in that boat?

Mr. ROSTRON. I have not the faintest idea.

Senator SMITH. Do you remember the number of men in the other boats?

Mr. ROSTRON. I can give you no details of the seamen or anything else. Remember one thing: Unless the sailors were dressed in some distinctive uniform, I could not tell the seamen, firemen, stewards, or passengers.

Senator NEWLANDS. When your ship arrived in New York, were any of the passengers dangerously ill?

Mr. ROSTRON. Not to my knowledge.

Senator NEWLANDS. How many died after you rescued them?

Mr. ROSTRON. None. No passengers died. Only the one seaman.

Senator SMITH. Do you know who took the lifeboats from the Carpathia?

Mr. ROSTRON. No.

Senator SMITH. It was probably done by the owners?

Mr. ROSTRON. No; I had previously to this sent a wireless to the White Star Line asking them to send a couple of tugboats down to quarantine to take these boats away, as I would not be able to come into dock with those boats up in the davits or on the forecastle head. There were none there, and so I was worrying about these. It was a dirty night, coming up the river last night, and I was worrying about what I was going to do with the boats. I had the boats lowered half way to the water, to avoid any waste of time. When we got right off the dock, I asked them to send some tugboats out to take the boats away, as I could not dock until they were gotten out of the way. After that I do not know anything about them.

Senator SMITH. Some complaint has been made because the message of the President of the United States, which was sent the Carpathia, was not answered. Do you know anything about that?

Mr. ROSTRON. I heard last night that there was a message about a Maj. Butt. I asked my purser this morning if he remembers any message asking if Maj. Butt was on board, and it was answered: "Not on board." That is the only thing I know about that message of that name. I do not remember anything else.

Senator SMITH. Was there any attempt to communicate with the Carpathia from any Government vessel?

Mr. ROSTRON. Yes; from the Chester. I got a message from the Chester. The exact words of it I quite forget now; but there was something in it about the President; something, as far as I remember, about his being anxious about the passengers, if I remember right. I was rather worried at the time, as it was foggy, and these messages came up to me on the bridge. I had my hands

60

full. He gave me his position and told me he was coming to take the names of the passengers and wanted my position. I answered him with my position and asked him if he could take the passengers names.

I told him the names of the first and second cabin passengers and crew had already gone. I said: "Can you take third-class names now?" I got a reply back: "Yes, yes."

Senator SMITH. From the Chester?

Mr. ROSTRON. From the Chester. Those are the two messages I got from the Chester.

Senator SMITH. Was there any attempt made by anyone to influence you in sending or receiving wireless messages?

Mr. ROSTRON. From the very commencement I took charge of the whole thing and issued orders that every message sent would be sent under my authority, and no message was to be sent unless authorized by me. My orders were: First of all, the two official messages. The two official messages were to the Cunard Co. and the White Star Co., as regards the accident, telling them that I had got an approximate number of passengers aboard and was returning to New York. That was to the White Star Co., and the other one was to our company, of course, telling them that I was proceeding to New York unless otherwise ordered, and considered New York the best, for many considerations.

After those two messages were sent, I sent a press message to the Associated Press, practically in the same words as I had sent to the companies, over my signature.

Those were the three first messages that were sent. After these messages were sent, we began sending in the names of the first-class passengers. This was by the Olympic on Monday evening. We got the first, and I think all the second off by the Olympic. Then we lost touch.

Senator SMITH. You lost touch?

Mr. ROSTRON. We lost touch; yes.

Senator SMITH. When was that?

Mr. ROSTRON. The hour I could not tell you. It was Tuesday morning some time very early in the morning, between 1 and 2 I think.

Senator SMITH. How many operators did you have on the Carpathia?

Mr. ROSTRON. One.

Senator SMITH. Was he in constant service from the time you received this first message from the Titanic?

Mr. ROSTRON. He was constantly at his instrument, the whole time.

Senator SMITH. How old a man was he?

Mr. ROSTRON. He is a young man. I should think he is about 25 years old.

Senator SMITH. Under whose employ?

Mr. ROSTRON. The Marconi Co.

Senator SMITH. What is his name?

Mr. ROSTRON. I can not tell you. I do not know his name.

Senator SMITH. Did you know, of your own knowledge, of the attempt of the President of the United States to communicate directly with your ship?

Mr. ROSTRON. Absolutely not; nothing whatever of that.

Senator SMITH. I guess that there was no intention whatever of either ignoring his message -

Mr. ROSTRON. (interposing). My word, I hope not, sir.

Senator SMITH. (continuing.). Or neglecting it?

Mr. ROSTRON. Absolutely no intention of any such thing, sir. It never entered the minds of anyone.

Senator SMITH. And no one attempted in any way to put a censorship over the wireless service on your ship?

Mr. ROSTRON. Absolutely no censorship whatever. I controlled the whole thing, through my orders. I said I placed official messages first. After they had gone, and the first press message, then the names of the passengers. After the names of the passengers and crew had been sent my orders were to send all private messages from the Titanic's passengers first in the order in which they were given in to the purser; no preference to any message.

Senator SMITH. You picked up a message from the Californian, did you not?

Mr. ROSTRON. No, we did not pick up a message. Wait a minute. We knew the Californian was about, because the operator had told me he had heard the Californian reply to those signals. That is all.

At 8 o'clock in the morning he hove in sight. This was at the wreck, and I left him when I returned to New York at 8.50, I think it was, when I put on full speed to come back. He was searching the vicinity of the wreckage, and I left for New York.

The next day I got a message from the Californian saying:

Have searched position carefully up to noon and found nothing and seen no bodies.

Senator SMITH. Did your wireless work right up to the time you intended to use it last?

Mr. ROSTRON. I do not follow your question, sir.

Senator SMITH. Did your wireless fail you at all?

Mr. ROSTRON. Never. The only thing is that we were not fitted up with a long-distance installation. It is only a short-distance outfit, for what we call ship messages, and close to land stations.

Senator SMITH. How far can you communicate? [using the Carpathia's short-range wireless]?

Mr. ROSTRON. Under good conditions, 200 miles. We only reckon, under ordinary conditions, on 150 miles. Fog, mist, haze, snow, or any other unfavorable weather conditions make it so that we may not get more than 90 to 100 miles.

Senator SMITH. It was rather accidental, then, that you happened to be within the radius of your instrument when you got the Titanic?

Mr. ROSTRON. Yes; we were only 58 miles away from them.

Senator SMITH. It was providential?

Mr. ROSTRON. The whole thing was absolutely providential. I will tell you this, that the wireless operator was in his cabin, at the time, not on official business at all, but just simply listening as he was undressing. He was unlacing his boots at the time. He had this apparatus on his ear, and the message came. That was the whole thing. In 10 minutes, maybe he would have been in bed, and we would not have heard the messages.

Senator SMITH. It was a very remarkable coincidence

Mr. ROSTRON. It was very remarkable, and, as I say, the whole thing was providential, as regards our being able to get there.

Mr. UHLER. You could receive from a long distance, but you could not send a response?

Mr. ROSTRON. We can always take from a long distance, yes.

Mr. UHLER. You have a low powered machine?

Mr. ROSTRON. Yes.

Senator SMITH. From what you have heard from the passengers or crew of the Titanic, do you know whether any of them saw the Titanic sink finally?

Mr. ROSTRON. Yes, several of the passengers to whom I have spoken saw the ship sink.

Senator SMITH. Do you remember who they were?

Mr. ROSTRON. I think Mrs. Thayer was one.

Senator SMITH. Mrs. J. B. Thayer?

Mr. ROSTRON. Yes; and her son Jack; and Mrs. Wagner.

Senator SMITH. And Col. Gracie?

Mr. ROSTRON. I do not remember. I do not know the names of any of the people who were saved. I never came across them.

Senator SMITH. You never talked with them?

Mr. ROSTRON. I had no opportunity to do so.

Senator SMITH. You were kept very busy?

Mr. ROSTRON. Yes.

Senator NEWLANDS. Captain, how many more lifeboats could you accommodate on the Carpathia than you have now?

Mr. ROSTRON. Under the present conditions, and of course if they were ordinary lifeboats, I do not believe we could take more than six, at the very outside. Of course, that is absolutely lumbering the deck up as it is.

Senator NEWLANDS. It would be lumbering the deck up, and you would only have space for 26 in all?

Mr. ROSTRON. Yes.

Senator NEWLANDS. And that would lumber up the deck to some extent?

Mr. ROSTRON. Yes. Not the passenger decks. It has nothing to do with the passenger decks. It would be the deck space that is not utilized by the passengers that would be lumbered up, not the promenade decks.

Senator NEWLANDS. I see. Would that additional number work much additional inconvenience upon the deck?

Mr. ROSTRON. No; I do not think so.

Senator NEWLANDS. Take the case of the Titanic, whose tonnage was more than three times as great as that of the Carpathia, which had, I believe, the same number of lifeboats as the Carpathia?

Mr. ROSTRON. Yes, sir.

Senator NEWLANDS. How many additional lifeboats could that vessel accommodate without inconvenience?

Mr. ROSTRON. I have not the faintest idea, sir, what the Titanic was like. I believe she is a sister ship of the Olympic. I have seen the Olympic once, when she was at the end of our dock. I have no idea of her construction. That is all I have seen of her.

Senator NEWLANDS. You think she could accommodate considerably more, do you not?

Mr. ROSTRON. If she could not accommodate them she could be made to accommodate them. If they build the ship knowing that she is only to carry 16 lifeboats they will utilize the space otherwise.

Senator NEWLANDS. How do you account for the fact that the Board of Trade of England, as the size of these ships has increased, has not compelled an increase in the number of life boats? Your maximum, as I understand, is 20 boats, is it not?

Mr. ROSTRON. Yes, I believe it is. But they have compelled a different construction of the ship itself. That is where the thing has come in.

Senator NEWLANDS. You regard each ship itself as a lifeboat?

Mr. ROSTRON. Yes, sir.

Senator NEWLANDS. That expectation was not realized in the case of this ship?

Mr. ROSTRON. It has been an abnormal experience as regards the Titanic.

Senator SMITH. Have you any kind of knowledge at all regarding the force of the impact which wrecked the Titanic?

Mr. ROSTRON. I know nothing about it, sir. I have not asked any questions about this kind of business. I knew it was not my affair, and I had little desire to make any of the officers feel it any more than they did. Mind you sir, there is only this: I know nothing, but I have heard rumors of different passengers; some will say one thing and some another. I would, therefore, rather say nothing. I do not know anything. From the officers I know nothing. I could give you silly rumors of passengers, but I know they are not reliable, from my own experience; so, if you will excuse me, I would prefer to say nothing.

Senator SMITH. I think that is all, Captain, and I want to thank you for your courtesy in appearing before the committee and giving us the information at your disposal..

Senator NEWLANDS. As to the equipment of these lifeboats, what are the requirements as to food and compass, and so on?

Mr. ROSTRON. They are all supplied with compass, and with water breakers and with bread tanks.

Mr. UHLER. And with mast and sail?

Mr. ROSTRON. And with mast and sail.

Mr. UHLER. And gear?

Mr. ROSTRON. And all of the necessary gear.

Senator NEWLANDS. Do you know whether those conditions were complied with with reference to these boats on the Titanic?

Mr. ROSTRON. As far as I can see, yes. I can tell you this, that I saw myself both water and biscuits in the boats, not all, of course, but one or two where the men were working about when we secured them. We put them on board our ship and we had to secure them, and under certain circumstances, we had to come up against the boat and look into them, and there were two or three boats where I did see both water and bread in the boats; and all of the boats had the bread tanks. That I know for certain. And they also had water breakers.

Senator SMITH. We are very much obliged to you, Capt. Rostron.

Mr. ROSTRON. You are quite welcome, sir. If there is anything further I can do, I shall be very glad.

Senator SMITH. After the recess I should like to have Mr. Marconi appear before us for a few minutes.

Mr. MARCONI. I shall be very glad to do so, Senator.

Senator SMITH. And the operator.

Mr. GRIGGS. He will be here by 3 o'clock, Senator.

Senator SMITH. That is, the operator from the Carpathia. Also the operator from the Titanic.

Mr. GRIGGS. He is not able to come. I am afraid the committee will have to go to him.

Mr. ROSTRON. Both his ankles and back are injured, although the last two days he was carried up in the Marconi operating room of the Carpathia to assist our operator all he could.

STATEMENT OF GUGLIELMO MARCONI.

Chairman, British Marconi Company

Senator SMITH. Mr. Marconi, will you give the reporter your full name?

Mr. MARCONI. Guglielmo Marconi.

Senator SMITH. State your place of residence, please.

Mr. MARCONI. London, England.

Senator SMITH. Your vocation?

Mr. MARCONI. Electrical engineer and chairman of the British Marconi Co.

Senator SMITH. As chairman of the British Marconi Co., have you men employed in wireless telegraphy?

Mr. MARCONI. Yes; a great number.

Senator SMITH. Did you have one of your employees on the Carpathia?

Mr. MARCONI. Yes, sir.

Senator SMITH. When she went to the rescue of the survivors of the Titanic?

Mr. MARCONI. Yes, sir.

Senator SMITH. What was his name?

Mr. MARCONI. I believe it is Cottam. I only met this man last night. I do not know how his name is spelled exactly. Cottam, I think. He is here.

Senator SMITH. In the establishment of the wireless service on boats of that character, is it done under the direction of your company?

Mr. MARCONI. Yes, sir.

Senator SMITH. Is the operator responsible to your company?

Mr. MARCONI. He is responsible in so far as the commercial work goes - as to accounting for messages and the general conduction of a commercial telegraphic service.

Senator SMITH. From whom does he receive instructions as to his hours of labor and his general work in that capacity aboard ship?

Mr. MARCONI. From the captain, according to the exigencies of the service.

Senator SMITH. Have you any specific instructions that he is called upon to observe in the performance of his duty?

Mr. MARCONI. Yes, there are numerous instructions which are general rules and regulations for expediting the traffic and for preventing interference with other ships.

Senator SMITH. Can you state briefly what those instructions are?

Mr. MARCONI. They are, in the main, the same rules and regulations as are enacted by the International Convention on Wireless Telegraphy.

Senator SMITH. Known as the Berlin treaty?

Mr. MARCONI. Known as the Berlin treaty, to which Great Britain is a party.

Senator SMITH. The United States is not yet a party?

Mr. MARCONI. It is not yet effectively a party, I understand.

Senator SMITH. The regulations of the international convention are the basis of your regulations and instructions to your men?

Mr. MARCONI. Yes, absolutely.

Senator SMITH. On shipboard must the operator take his instructions as to the hours of labor from the captain of the ship?

Mr. MARCONI. Yes.

Senator SMITH. Under these instructions are you required to have more than one operator on a ship making a voyage of this character?

Mr. MARCONI. No - it depends. If the ship is a large one, usually two operators are supplied.

Senator SMITH. Do you mean the supplying of two operators depends upon the size of the ship or upon the character of the apparatus?

Mr. MARCONI. I mean if it is a large ship like the Titanic, the Olympic, the Mauretania, or the Lusitania they always carry two operators, but the smaller ships of the class or size of the Carpathia carry one.

Senator SMITH. When you refer to large or small ships, do you refer to the matter of tonnage or to the matter of passenger room?

Mr. MARCONI. I refer to the average number of passengers carried. The number carried or the number for whom accommodation is provided. We generally presume that a ship with large passenger accommodations will carry a greater number of passengers.

Senator SMITH. Was any effort made, to your knowledge, to increase the number of operators on the Carpathia?

Mr. MARCONI. It was not considered necessary, and the shipowners did not consider it necessary either so far as I am aware.

Senator SMITH. With what kind of wireless service or equipment is the Carpathia provided?

Mr. MARCONI. The Carpathia is provided with an equipment which I should call a short-distance equipment; it is an apparatus which can transmit messages, under favorable circumstances, up to about 180 or 200 miles. On the average I should say the distance is about 100 miles.

Senator SMITH. Does this depend upon the weather or the sea?

Mr. MARCONI. It depends on numerous circumstances. It depends on the state of space; not necessarily the apparent weather. It may be a very bad day and still the messages may go all right. It also depends to a large extent on the skill of the operator.

Senator SMITH. As to the distance within which communication may be effected?

Mr. MARCONI. Yes. If he can adjust his transmitter to its best condition, approaching its greatest efficiency, he will effect communication at the greatest distance.

Senator SMITH. Referring to the equipment on the Carpathia, its maximum efficiency would be about 180 miles?

Mr. MARCONI. I should say perhaps 200.

Senator SMITH. Two hundred miles?

Mr. MARCONI. Sometimes perhaps more, but on very rare occasions.

Senator SMITH. Do you know about the equipment of the Titanic?

Mr. MARCONI. Yes.

Senator SMITH. Was the Titanic equipped by your company?

Mr. MARCONI. The Titanic was equipped by my company.

Senator SMITH. I wish you would describe the wireless equipment of the Titanic, stating the character of the apparatus and how modern and powerful it was.

Mr. MARCONI. The wireless equipment on the Titanic was a fairly powerful set, capable, I should say, of communicating four or five hundred miles during the daytime and much further during the nighttime.

Senator SMITH. How much further at nighttime?

Mr. MARCONI. Very often a thousand miles. I should say almost every night 1,000 miles.

Senator SMITH. With accuracy?

Mr. MARCONI. With accuracy.

Senator SMITH. Would you say that the Titanic was equipped with the latest and best wireless apparatus?

Mr. MARCONI. Yes. I should say it was the latest apparatus for that purpose.

Senator SMITH. Did the company, of which you are the president, designate the operators for the Titanic?

Mr. MARCONI. Do you mean did it choose the operators for the Titanic?

Senator SMITH. Yes; or assign them?

Mr. MARCONI. They assign them generally in consultation with the shipping companies. They consult the shipping companies in regard to them.

Senator SMITH. What is the ordinary pay for a wireless telegrapher?

Mr. MARCONI. In England, on British ships, I think they commence about 30 shillings a week, and they go up to over £ 2 per week. In addition to that, they get their board and lodging. I am speaking now subject to some error, because it is some time since I have been directly connected with those matters. I have a managing director who attend the question of salaries.

Senator SMITH. Your statement is correct, as far as you have made it?

Mr. MARCONI. Yes, sir.

Senator SMITH. In America what is the wage?

Mr. MARCONI. I am not aware of the exact wage paid in America. An official of the American company is present, and he would be able give you an accurate reply.

Senator SMITH. How many operators were on the Titanic?

Mr. MARCONI. I believe there were two.

Senator SMITH. Did they both survive, do you know?

Mr. MARCONI. No, sir. One was drowned; died. He was the chief operator, I am informed.

Senator SMITH. And the other?

Mr. MARCONI. And the other was picked up, I believe. He got on a raft, on a collapsible boat, and he was rescued by the Carpathia, having been wounded in his ankles or his legs.

Senator SMITH. At any time during Sunday last, were your offices here in communication with the Titanic?

Mr. MARCONI. I can not answer that, but I can produce a person who can.

Senator SMITH. Have you been in communication with the Carpathia since the disaster to the Titanic?

Mr. MARCONI. I believe so, at least a great number of messages have come through from the Carpathia to my knowledge. I sent no message to the Carpathia, nor did I receive any.

Senator SMITH. Did your company?

Mr. MARCONI. My company has.

Senator SMITH. Your company has received no messages?

Mr. MARCONI. Yes; my company I believe has.

Senator SMITH. It has both sent and received messages?

Mr. MARCONI. I believe so; I have no personal knowledge, but I think they have.

Senator SMITH. Would you say from what you know about the receipt of messages sent from and to the ship that the wireless was working fairly well?

Mr. MARCONI. I believe it was working fairly well.

Senator SMITH. You believe it was in good order?

Mr. MARCONI. In good order; yes.

Senator SMITH. Where is the operator of the Titanic who survived?

Mr. MARCONI. The operator of the Titanic is on another Cunard boat; I believe at the dock; I think the Saxonia. He has been removed there, but he is unable to walk in consequence of the injury to his ankles.

Senator SMITH. He has not been in the hospital?

Mr. MARCONI. No; I do not think he has.

Senator SMITH. What boat did you say he was on?

Mr. MARCONI. I think the Saxonia.

Senator SMITH. Do you know why he is on the Saxonia?

Mr. MARCONI. Because the Carpathia was to have sailed.

Senator SMITH. To-day?

Mr. MARCONI. To-day; and of course he did not belong to the Carpathia. He was just on board.

Senator SMITH. When does the Saxonia sail?

Mr. MARCONI. I do not know.

Senator SMITH. It is not the intention of this operator to return to England immediately, is it?

Mr. MARCONI. No; I do not think it is, and it is not my intention either, that he should leave.

Senator SMITH. Have you any authority over him?

Mr. MARCONI. I have the authority that the president of a company has over one of the employees.

Senator SMITH. May I request you to have him remain and present himself to the committee as soon as agreeable?

Mr. MARCONI. Yes sir; I shall be very glad to instruct him to that effect.

Senator SMITH. Where is the operator of the Carpathia?

Mr. MARCONI. The operator of the Carpathia was instructed to be here at 3 o'clock.

Senator SMITH. Is he here?

Mr. MARCONI. I do not see him. We might have him called. Cottam is his name.

Mr. JOHN W. GRIGGS. He is not here

Mr. MARCONI. He went on board ship to take his clothes off.

Senator SMITH. And will be back here?

Mr. MARCONI. He should be back here now.

Senator SMITH. I wish you would also ask him to remain.

Mr. MARCONI. Yes, sir.

Mr. GRIGGS. Mr. Chairman, if you would allow me, I wish to say that the operator of the Carpathia as well as the assistant operator of the Titanic have been detained at the instruction of the officers of the company for the purpose of being at the service of this committee.

Senator SMITH. I understand that, Governor.

Mr. GRIGGS. They will be detained as long as is necessary for this committee to hear them. With reference to the one from the Titanic, I doubt very much whether he can be removed from his present quarters without great inconvenience.

Senator SMITH. I understand, Governor, from the officers that that is their disposition, but this being the president of the Marconi Co., I thought I would like to get into the record his affirmative promise that that should be done.

Mr. MARCONI. Perhaps I should make one explanation. When I say I am the president of the Marconi Co. these operators are really in the employ of a subsidiary company of what we call the Marconi Co., but this company is controlled by the company of which I am the chairman.

Senator SMITH. But it is sufficient to say that you feel that you have influence enough to carry out the wishes of the committee?

Mr. MARCONI. Yes, sir.

Senator SMITH. I want to know if you can tell me from your own knowledge whether there was any general interference from the time this collision occurred at sea on the part of experimental or rival service to the detriment of this service.

Mr. MARCONI. I should say, if you will allow me, that I have only seen these operators for a few minutes; and not having been there, I can not give a very definite answer to that question. They, no doubt, will be able to reply to it fully, but in so far as my impression goes, it is that near New York there was some slight interference, but at a distance from New York, when the Carpathia was communicating with stations in Long Island and in Nova Scotia, there was practically no interference.

Senator SMITH. Can you tell me how wide an area was communicated with from the Carpathia, generally speaking - considering, for instance, a wireless of the character you describe?

Mr. MARCONI. Yes.

Senator SMITH. And put them in communication with your office here. In the course of that message, how far from its original point of destination would a message of that kind extend?

Mr. MARCONI. Of course, the message, I should say, does not come direct to our office.

Senator SMITH. Well, to your -

Mr. MARCONI. It is taken on a coast station.

Senator SMITH. To your coast station, then.

Mr. MARCONI. Then it is sent on by wire to the office.

Senator SMITH. When I referred to your office, I meant coast station.

Mr. MARCONI. The wireless message, or the waves of ships equipped in the way that the Carpathia is equipped, would affect a space which is that contained in a circle of the diameter of three or four hundred miles. The radius of the station being 200 miles, it will affect a space of 200 miles all around. I am now talking about the maximum range.

Senator SMITH. Then interference would be quite possible?

Mr. MARCONI. Interference would be quite possible, assuming that interferent stations or parties were using the same wave length as the Carpathia. Fortunately they use different wave lengths; and you can not interfere while using different wave lengths.

Senator SMITH. What wave length would be required on such a communication as the Carpathia first made to your shore stations?

Mr. MARCONI. I should say they were using a 600-meter wave, which is one of the international convention waves. I have not the information in regard to that, but I assume it.

Senator SMITH. Is that the minimum of the international convention?

Mr. MARCONI. No; it is the longest.

Senator SMITH. I mean the maximum.

Mr. MARCONI. Yes, sir; the maximum. The shortest is 300.

Senator SMITH. And the minimum is 300?

Mr. MARCONI. Yes.

Senator SMITH. This was the maximum wave length -

Mr. MARCONI. Yes.

Senator SMITH. Prescribed by the international convention?

Mr. MARCONI. Yes, sir.

Senator SMITH. Would the instrument of the Carpathia have been able to send a greater wave length than 600?

Mr. MARCONI. I do not think so.

Senator SMITH. Did you hear the captain of the Carpathia testify?

Mr. MARCONI. I heard the end of his evidence; just the latter part.

Senator SMITH. Did you hear him say that they caught this message from the Titanic providentially?

Mr. MARCONI. I heard him say that.

Senator SMITH. That the operator was removing his shoes and about to retire?

Mr. MARCONI. Yes, sir; I quite admit that it was providential.

Senator SMITH. And that in five minutes more communication would have been impossible?

Mr. MARCONI. It was absolutely providential. I agree with the captain.

Senator SMITH. If this operator is not at his post of duty, has the wireless message no signal to arouse him?

Mr. MARCONI. Not the way it is installed on most boats.

Senator SMITH. Did it have on this boat?

Mr. MARCONI. It had not, so far as I am aware.

Senator SMITH. Did it have it on the Titanic?

Mr. MARCONI. I do not think so.

Senator SMITH. So that it is absolutely necessary that the operator should be at his post all the time in order to facilitate or give effect to communications from ships or coast stations?

Mr. MARCONI. Yes, sir; or ships in distress, I should say.

Senator SMITH. Ships in distress and coast stations?

Mr. MARCONI. And coast stations. Of course, if a coast station or ship calls another ship and the operator does not answer, he simply waits until later, till the operator is awake or until he has come back. I am referring to the ordinary commercial communications.

Senator SMITH. Yes, but later in this instance would have probably meant that all these passengers and crew that were saved would have been lost.

Mr. MARCONI. Yes, sir; I quite admit that.

Senator SMITH. Do you recall any international regulations of the Berlin convention or any provision relating to that matter?

Mr. MARCONI. I do not think there is any provision in regard to that matter.

Senator SMITH. Ought it not be incumbent upon ships at sea who have the wireless apparatus to have an operator always at his key?

Mr. MARCONI. I think it certainly should be. Of course, it might come rather hard on small ships. The shipowners will not like the expense of two men.

Senator SMITH. On the English basis of wage it would not be very serious?

Mr. MARCONI. No; it would not be, but it is very much a matter that affects the shipowners; they do not like to carry two operators when they can get along with one.

Senator SMITH. On the Titanic, if you know, was there a constant relay?

Mr. MARCONI. You mean a constant lookout? Constant attention?

Senator SMITH. Yes.

Mr. MARCONI. Yes; there should be and there was.

Senator SMITH. That was the purpose of having two operators?

Mr. MARCONI. That was the purpose of having two operators, and also for the purpose of handling the greater number of messages which come to a larger and more important ship.

Senator SMITH. Are those men of equal skill?

Mr. MARCONI. Usually there is one man in charge who is an experienced man, and the other man is also a telegraphist, but a junior man of less experience.

Senator SMITH. And less remuneration?

Mr. MARCONI. Yes, sir. I should, if you will allow me, to state that all the wireless telegraphists employed on British ships have to get a license of competency from the English Government, or they are not allowed to operate.

Senator SMITH. Does that go to their competency as operators?

Mr. MARCONI. I think it does.

Senator SMITH. Does it include their character as man?

Mr. MARCONI. Yes, sir.

Senator SMITH. And general fitness?

Mr. MARCONI. And general fitness.

Senator SMITH. Do you have much difficulty in supplying your stations with operators?

Mr. MARCONI. Sometimes we have. It takes some time to train them. We train them at a school of ours.

Senator SMITH. Do you have any regulations that touch the question of their habits?

Mr. MARCONI. They have to be subject to the discipline of the ship. They must obey the captain, as everyone aboard a ship has to do, and of course they have to behave in a decent manner on shore. They must not discredit the service in any way.

Senator SMITH. I should like to ask whether, in your opinion, the amateur operators of wireless stations are calculated to minimize the effectiveness of practical work on land and sea?

Mr. MARCONI. I think it does effectively minimize or hamper the useful communications, because on an occasion like this I was told - I always want confirmation from a man who was there - but, if I remember correctly, I was told last night that a great number of unknown stations called up the captain for news.

Senator SMITH. Unknown stations?

Mr. MARCONI. Yes, sir. Of course the ship would not reply except to the authorized stations sending traffic. That causes interference and causes trouble.

In England, of course, that is impossible, because stations are not allowed to do that.

Senator SMITH. How long has wireless telegraphy been a practical science?

Mr. MARCONI. I think it has been a practical science since - you mean in regard to shipping?

Senator SMITH. In regard to shipping.

Mr. MARCONI. I should say since 1900. Of course, great improvements have been made since.

Senator SMITH. Who made the first successful experiment?

Mr. MARCONI. On ships?

Senator SMITH. Yes.

Mr. MARCONI. I think I did myself.

Senator SMITH. In what year?

Mr. MARCONI. In 1897.

Senator SMITH. Since that time have you have found it efficient in cases of a similar character?

Mr. MARCONI. To that of the Titanic and Carpathia. Yes; I am very glad to say that it has been of paramount utility in a great number of cases.

Senator SMITH. In what cases?

Mr. MARCONI. The most important, looking backward, was the collision, which occurred between the Republic, of the White Star Line, and the Florida, near Nantucket; when assistance was summoned; and, fortunately, in that case practically everyone was saved.

Other cases have occurred with other ships. I remember a lightship in the English Channel which was run down over 10 years ago which obtained assistance by the same means; and one of the Cunard liners got into trouble some time ago - a long time ago - and summoned assistance by the same methods. Of course the two important and sensational cases in which it has proved of utility have been the wreck of the Republic, and this disaster to the Titanic.

Senator SMITH. Do you regard the Berlin convention as a step in the direction of the international utility of wireless telegraphy?

Mr. MARCONI. I think in regard to shipping and shore stations it is a good regulation. It is a means for regulating the working and preventing interference; provided, however, that it is administered in a fair manner by the Governments concerned.

Senator SMITH. How many wireless stations are there now in the United States; do you know?

Mr. MARCONI. I do not know exactly, but there is a fair number.

Senator SMITH. What is the maximum distance over which communications may be accurately made?

Mr. MARCONI. The longest distance I can recall is from Ireland to the Argentine Republic.

Senator SMITH. From where?

Mr. MARCONI. Ireland.

Senator SMITH. From what point?

Mr. MARCONI. Clifton, Ireland, to Buenos Aires.

Senator SMITH. In the Argentine Republic?

Mr. MARCONI. Yes; in the Argentine Republic. That is 6,000 miles.

Senator SMITH. Have you personal knowledge of the correctness of that?

Mr. MARCONI. I have personal knowledge, because I was at the receiving end when the message was received.

Senator SMITH. You were at the receiving end?

Mr. MARCONI. I was in South America, at Buenos Aires. My assistants were in Ireland.

Senator SMITH. What wave length was used in that test?

Mr. MARCONI. A wave length between 7,000 and 8,000 meters, 25,000 feet.

Senator SMITH. In that test was there any mountainous obstructions?

Mr. MARCONI. There was a part of the coast of Brazil intervening between the two.

Senator SMITH. And that is mountainous?

Mr. MARCONI. That is mountainous in that part.

Senator SMITH. Was the Californian equipped with wireless?

Mr. MARCONI. I do not know.

Senator SMITH. It was not equipped by you?

Mr. MARCONI. I could not say one way or the other. I should say that I travel about a great deal and ships are equipped in England when I am not there.

Senator SMITH. Have you made any experiments in transoceanic service of that character?

Mr. MARCONI. Yes, sir. It is employed at present for transmitting messages between Canada and Ireland, a place called Glace Bay in Canada, and another place called Clifton, in Ireland.

Senator SMITH. Is that assuming a practical phase?

Mr. MARCONI. That is on a practical and commercial basis, the distance being approximately 2,000 miles between the two points.

Senator SMITH. What wave length is required?

Mr. MARCONI. The wave length there is 7,000 meters.

Senator SMITH. When was that communication between Ireland and Buenos Aires?

Mr. MARCONI. It was in October, in 1910.

Senator SMITH. Is there any proficiency test prescribed by any special board in England?

Mr. MARCONI. Yes; the operators have to pass a proficiency test before the post office authorities, which control the telegraphs in England.

Senator SMITH. Is there any in this country?

Mr. MARCONI. I believe there is now.

Senator SMITH. How recently?

Mr. MARCONI. Since a law was passed compelling passenger-carrying vessels to carry wireless-telegraph apparatus.

Senator SMITH. About two years ago?

Mr. MARCONI. About two years ago.

Senator SMITH. There seems to be a distinction between commercial business and distress or emergency business, ships business. Why should that be so?

Mr. MARCONI. For this reason: The commercial business is paid for and accounted for between the ships and the shore stations and organizations working the telegraphs on land, whilst, of course, for distress messages and messages affecting the safety of ships no charge is made and is not in itself a commercial business.

Senator SMITH. The Berlin convention, however, rather exalts the emergency phase of wireless telegraphy, giving to distress calls the precedence over all other calls, does it not?

Mr. MARCONI. Yes, sir; it has copied us in that, because that was one of our provisions before there was any Berlin convention.

Senator SMITH. It even takes precedence of Government business, does it not?

Mr. MARCONI. Even of Government business; yes.

Senator SMITH. Mr. Marconi, were any orders given by the Marconi Co., to the operators or the operator on the Carpathia, with reference to the receipt and answer of messages?

Mr. MARCONI. None whatever.

Senator SMITH. Do you know anything about the effort of the President of the United States to communicate with the Carpathia?

Mr. MARCONI. Except what I have read in the newspapers.

Senator SMITH. But, so far as you know, there was no disposition to censorize or control the operator of the Carpathia.

Mr. MARCONI. There was none whatever; and further, I was very much surprised at the things that were stated in the press, that a reply had been refused or had not been transmitted.

Senator SMITH. Do you know whether there was a reply refused?

Mr. MARCONI. Only from what I saw in the press. I might say that the operator, of course, can speak for himself; but I asked him that question last night when I boarded the Carpathia and he told me that he never dreamed of refusing to reply to a message sent by the President.

Senator SMITH.   I think that is all. We are very much obliged to you.

TESTIMONY OF CHARLES HERBERT LIGHTOLLER.

Second Officer, SS Titanic

Mr. Lightoller was sworn by the chairman.

Senator SMITH. What is your name?

Mr. LIGHTOLLER. Charles Herbert Lightoller.

Senator SMITH. Mr. Lightoller, where do you reside?

Mr. LIGHTOLLER. Netley Abbey, Hampshire.

Senator SMITH. England?

Mr. LIGHTOLLER. England.

Senator SMITH. How old are you?

Mr. LIGHTOLLER. Thirty-eight.

Senator SMITH. What is your business?

Mr. LIGHTOLLER. Seaman.

Senator SMITH. How long have you been in the service or employment?

Mr. LIGHTOLLER. Thirteen years and three months.

Senator SMITH. How extensive has been your service in that time?

Mr. LIGHTOLLER. I do not quite follow you.

Senator SMITH. How much service have you seen? In what capacities?

Mr. LIGHTOLLER. In all the capacities in the White Star service - fourth, third, second, and first officer.

Senator SMITH. You have been in the White Star service during all of that time?

Mr. LIGHTOLLER. Yes, sir.

Senator SMITH. What official positions have you held?

Mr. LIGHTOLLER. Fourth, third, second, and first officer.

Senator SMITH. What position do you occupy now?

Mr. LIGHTOLLER. Second officer of the Titanic.

Senator SMITH. How long have you been second officer?

Mr. LIGHTOLLER. Altogether, about seven years.

Senator SMITH. When did you go aboard the Titanic?

Mr. LIGHTOLLER. In Belfast.

Senator SMITH. When?

Mr. LIGHTOLLER. March 19 or 20.

Senator SMITH. Did you make the so-called trial trips?

Mr. LIGHTOLLER. Yes, sir.

Senator SMITH. Of what did they consist?

Mr. LIGHTOLLER. Turning circles and adjusting compasses.

Senator SMITH. In what waters?

Mr. LIGHTOLLER. Belfast Lough.

Senator SMITH. How extensive is that lough?

Mr. LIGHTOLLER. I can hardly say offhand without seeing a chart.

Senator SMITH. Have you any data here that shows?

Mr. LIGHTOLLER. No.

Senator SMITH. Just state as nearly as you can.

Mr. LIGHTOLLER. It may be about 15 miles long, widening out from a few miles wide to perhaps 7 miles. That is only approximate, sir.

Senator SMITH. Have you ever been in that water before?

Mr. LIGHTOLLER. Only passing through.

Senator SMITH. How did you happen to pass through it?

Mr. LIGHTOLLER. Going into Belfast or coming out bound to some port. I do not mean in an official capacity; as a passenger. I have been through it in an official capacity about 11 years ago.

Senator SMITH. Is that water usually selected for these trial tests for new ships?

Mr. LIGHTOLLER. Yes.

Senator SMITH. What was the condition of the weather when you made this trial test?

Mr. LIGHTOLLER. Light breeze, clear weather, sir.

Senator SMITH. From the time you boarded the Titanic did you at any time encounter any rough weather?

Mr. LIGHTOLLER. No, sir.

Senator SMITH. You were always in smooth water, so called?

Mr. LIGHTOLLER. Yes, sir.

Senator SMITH. Does that include up to the time of this collision?

Mr. LIGHTOLLER. Yes, sir.

Senator SMITH. Of what do these trial tests consist?

Mr. LIGHTOLLER. Turning circles.

Senator SMITH. I wish you would describe that a little more fully. Under what head of steam and how fast would the boat be moving?

Mr. LIGHTOLLER. Under various speeds.

Senator SMITH. In how large a radius would these circles be made?

Mr. LIGHTOLLER. Turning circles consists of seeing in what space the ship will turn under certain helms with the engines at various speeds.

Senator SMITH. Was this boat tested at its maximum speed?

Mr. LIGHTOLLER. That I could not say, sir.

Senator SMITH. What was the maximum speed of this boat?

Mr. LIGHTOLLER. That I could not say, sir. She was never put, to my knowledge, to her maximum speed.

Senator SMITH. What did you understand it to be?

Mr. LIGHTOLLER. About 22 1/2 to 23 knots.

Senator SMITH. From whom did you get that information?

Mr. LIGHTOLLER. General rumor, sir

Senator SMITH. Did you talk with the boat's officers?

Mr. LIGHTOLLER. From talk generally; yes. It was only an approximate idea.

Senator SMITH. How much time was spent in the test?

Mr. LIGHTOLLER. I could not say exactly.

Senator SMITH. Approximately?

Mr. LIGHTOLLER. About five hours.

Senator SMITH. During that time those circles were made?

Mr. LIGHTOLLER. Yes, sir.

Senator SMITH. And the ship reversed?

Mr. LIGHTOLLER. Yes, sir.

Senator SMITH. And put on a straight course?

Mr. LIGHTOLLER. Yes, sir.

Senator SMITH. And under full head?

Mr. LIGHTOLLER. I could not say, sir. She steamed for a certain distance under approximately a full head of steam; but how much steam was on I could not say, or what pressure of steam.

Senator SMITH. How many engines were there in this boat?

Mr. LIGHTOLLER. Two reciprocating and one turbine.

Senator SMITH. Were they all working on the trial test?

Mr. LIGHTOLLER. So far as I know, sir.

Senator SMITH. What do you know about that? Were you in the engine room?

Mr. LIGHTOLLER. No, sir; I was on my station, aft.

Senator SMITH. Where was your station?

Mr. LIGHTOLLER. The after end of the ship.

Senator SMITH. Then you would not, of your own knowledge, know whether its entire power was being tested out or not?

Mr. LIGHTOLLER. I should not; no, sir.

Senator SMITH. Five hours was the length of time spent in making those tests?

Mr. LIGHTOLLER. Approximately the length of time occupied in turning those circles.

Senator SMITH. What was the next thing that was done with the ship?

Mr. LIGHTOLLER. She was run a certain distance on a comparatively straight course and back again.

Senator SMITH. How far?

Mr. LIGHTOLLER. I could not say without a chart, sir.

Senator SMITH. How long did it take you?

Mr. LIGHTOLLER. Approximately four hours.

Senator SMITH. To make the straight run?

Mr. LIGHTOLLER. Yes, sir.

Senator SMITH. And return?

Mr. LIGHTOLLER. And return.

Senator SMITH. Four hours all together, two out and two back?

Mr. LIGHTOLLER. Two out and two back. That is only approximate.

Senator SMITH. Would you think from what you observed in the movements of this ship that it was going pretty fast?

Mr. LIGHTOLLER. For a ship of that size, a fair speed.

Senator SMITH. Fair speed?

Mr. LIGHTOLLER. A fair speed.

Senator SMITH. What would you call real good speed?

Mr. LIGHTOLLER. When the ship was built, we only expected her to go 21 knots, therefore all over 21 we thought very good.

Senator SMITH. This ship exceeded 21 knots?

Mr. LIGHTOLLER. On the trials? I am not speaking of the trials. I do not know what the speed was; I have no idea.

Senator SMITH. I understand you to say that you expected to get 21 knots out of her?

Mr. LIGHTOLLER. The builders, I presume, to get 21.

Senator SMITH. That was the general rumor?

Mr. LIGHTOLLER. Yes.

Senator SMITH. Among the officers?

Mr. LIGHTOLLER. Yes.

Senator SMITH. I suppose that was the hope, too, of the officers?

Mr. LIGHTOLLER. Exactly.

Senator SMITH. What boat had you been on before you went on board the Titanic?

Mr. LIGHTOLLER. The Oceanic.

Senator SMITH. The Oceanic, of the same line?

Mr. LIGHTOLLER. Of the same line.

Senator SMITH. How large a boat is the Oceanic?

Mr. LIGHTOLLER. Seventeen thousand tons gross.

Senator SMITH. Do you know her maximum speed?

Mr. LIGHTOLLER. Twenty-one knots.

Senator SMITH. I want to be sure I get the results of these trial tests accurately. I want you to tell me how long it took to make these tests. The straightaway tests and the circle tests altogether consumed how much time?

Mr. LIGHTOLLER. Approximately six or seven hours. I could not say any nearer than that.

Senator SMITH. What time of day did you begin these tests?

Mr. LIGHTOLLER. In the morning.

Senator SMITH. How early?

Mr. LIGHTOLLER. About 10 o'clock.

Senator SMITH. Was it clear weather?

Mr. LIGHTOLLER. Perfectly clear.

Senator SMITH. Was there any sea?

Mr. LIGHTOLLER. Very little.

Senator SMITH. And after about seven hours the tests were concluded?

Mr. LIGHTOLLER. With the exception of full speed astern; that is to see in what distance the ship will stop with the engines full speed astern - what we call the full speed astern test.

Senator SMITH. Was that made that day?

Mr. LIGHTOLLER. Yes, sir.

Senator SMITH. How long did that take?

Mr. LIGHTOLLER. That was only the matter of minutes.

Senator SMITH. A few minutes?

Mr. LIGHTOLLER. A few minutes.

Senator SMITH. Do you know who was aboard the Titanic in these trial tests?

Mr. LIGHTOLLER. A great number. I know some of them.

Senator SMITH. Please state those that you know.

Mr. LIGHTOLLER. Capt. Smith; Mr. Murdoch, chief officer; myself, first officer; Mr. Blair, second officer; Mr. Pitman, third officer; Mr. Boxhall, fourth officer; Mr. Lowe, fifth officer; Mr. Moody, sixth officer; and Mr. Andrews, of Harland & Wolff.

Senator SMITH. Representing the builders?

Mr. LIGHTOLLER. Yes, sir. I could not say anyone else with any accuracy.

Senator SMITH. Who was the chief engineer?

Mr. LIGHTOLLER. Mr. Bell, chief engineer; Mr. Ferguson, second engineer; Mr. Hesketh, also second. That is all I know.

Senator SMITH. How many men constituted the crew?

Mr. LIGHTOLLER. Seamen, you are speaking of?

Senator SMITH. Yes.

Mr. LIGHTOLLER. About 71 all told; officers and crew.

Senator SMITH. And seamen?

Mr. LIGHTOLLER. Yes, sir.

Senator SMITH. On the trial test?

Mr. LIGHTOLLER. Oh, no, sir. I am not speaking of the trial.

Senator SMITH. How many men constituted the crew on the trial tests?

Mr. LIGHTOLLER. About 30 of the crew and about 30 of what we call runners.

Senator SMITH. Were there any guests on the boat?

Mr. LIGHTOLLER. I believe there were; I could not say who.

Senator SMITH. Do you know who they were?

Mr. LIGHTOLLER. No, sir.

Senator SMITH. Were there any of the officers of the White Star Line?

Mr. LIGHTOLLER. I could not say with certainty, sir.

Senator SMITH. You do not recall seeing any of them?

Mr. LIGHTOLLER. I do not recall; no, sir. I believe there were some on board; but I can not remember who they were. I was not brought in contact with them.

Senator SMITH. Was Mr. Ismay aboard?

Mr. LIGHTOLLER. Not to my knowledge, sir.

Senator SMITH. Did you hear afterwards that he was on board?

Mr. LIGHTOLLER. No, sir.

Senator SMITH. You can not recall any officer of the company that was?

Mr. LIGHTOLLER. No, sir.

Senator SMITH. I mean any general officer?

Mr. LIGHTOLLER. No, sir.

Senator SMITH. Or director?

Mr. LIGHTOLLER. No, sir.

Senator SMITH. Was there anybody aboard representing the British Government?

Mr. LIGHTOLLER. Not to my knowledge, sir.

Senator SMITH. Were there any other officers of any other White Star Line boats?

Mr. LIGHTOLLER. No, sir.

Senator SMITH. After the final test, what was done with the boat?

Mr. LIGHTOLLER. We proceeded toward Southampton.

Senator SMITH. Immediately?

Mr. LIGHTOLLER. Almost immediately after taking on board a few things that had been left behind, which were required for the completion of the ship.

Senator SMITH. What?

Mr. LIGHTOLLER. So far as I know, requisites down in the galley, cooking apparatus, a few chairs, and such things as that.

Senator SMITH. Was the life-saving equipment -

Mr. LIGHTOLLER. Oh, no, sir; nothing like that.

Senator SMITH. Was the life-saving equipment complete?

Mr. LIGHTOLLER. Yes, sir.

Senator SMITH. Of what did it consist?

Mr. LIGHTOLLER. The necessary number of lifeboats.

Senator SMITH. I wish you would say how that is determined, if you can.

Mr. LIGHTOLLER. By the number of people on board.

Senator SMITH. You do not know how many there are on board until you are ready to start?

Mr. LIGHTOLLER. No sir.

Senator SMITH. Is it not determined by the number of accommodations rather than by the number of people who get aboard?

Mr. LIGHTOLLER. There must be life-saving apparatus for every one on board, regardless of accommodations.

Senator SMITH. Yes; but what I desire to know is whether in each stateroom on each deck, in all classes, whether there is any rule, and whether it was followed at that time, so far as you know, in equipping this boat with life preservers and life belts and anything else that might appropriately go into the rooms and be upon the decks of a boat of that character?

Mr. LIGHTOLLER. She was perfectly complete throughout, sir.

Senator SMITH. How many lifeboats were there?

Mr. LIGHTOLLER. Sixteen.

Senator SMITH. All of the same type?

Mr. LIGHTOLLER. Consisting of 14 lifeboats, 2 emergency boats, and 4 collapsible boats.

Senator SMITH. Tell us whether they were new entirely.

Mr. LIGHTOLLER. Entirely new.

Senator SMITH. And in their proper places?

Mr. LIGHTOLLER. In their proper places.

Senator SMITH. With the necessary lowering apparatus?

Mr. LIGHTOLLER. Everything complete, examined by the officers of the ship.

Senator SMITH. Was a test of the lifeboats made before you sailed for Southampton?

Mr. LIGHTOLLER. All the gear was tested.

Senator SMITH. Were the lifeboats lowered?

Mr. LIGHTOLLER. Yes, sir.

Senator SMITH. Under whose orders?

Mr. LIGHTOLLER. The officers, principally my orders.

Senator SMITH. Under your orders?

Mr. LIGHTOLLER. Yes.

Senator SMITH. Did you see the work done?

Mr. LIGHTOLLER. I did.

Senator SMITH. Tell just what was done.

Mr. LIGHTOLLER. All the boats on the ship were swung out and those that I required were lowered down as far as I wanted them - some all the way down, and some dropped into the water.

Senator SMITH. I wish you would give the proportion that went into the water.

Mr. LIGHTOLLER. About six.

Senator SMITH. Six into the water?

Mr. LIGHTOLLER. Yes.

Senator SMITH. And the others lowered?

Mr. LIGHTOLLER. Part of the way - as far as I thought necessary.

Senator SMITH. Part of the way?

Mr. LIGHTOLLER. Yes.

Senator SMITH. Of course, part of the way would not do anybody much good on a sinking ship. I assume you did that for the purpose of trying the gear, and not for the purpose of testing the security of the lifeboats?

Mr. LIGHTOLLER. It is principally the gear that we test. The lifeboats we know to be all right.

Senator SMITH. These boats were lowered from what deck?

Mr. LIGHTOLLER. From the boat deck.

Senator SMITH. Is that the sun deck?

Mr. LIGHTOLLER. That is the top deck.

Senator SMITH. Do you know how far it was from that top deck to the water?

Mr. LIGHTOLLER. Seventy feet.

Senator SMITH. What time did you reach Southampton?

Mr. LIGHTOLLER. About midnight.

Senator SMITH. Of what night?

Mr. LIGHTOLLER. I could not say.

Senator SMITH. Think it over.

Mr. LIGHTOLLER. I think it was the morning of the 4th of April.

Senator SMITH. What makes you think it was the morning of the 4th?

Mr. LIGHTOLLER. Because we sailed on the 10th.

Senator SMITH. How long did it take to make the run to Southampton?

Mr. LIGHTOLLER. About 24 hours.

Senator SMITH. Did you strike any heavy weather?

Mr. LIGHTOLLER. No, sir.

Senator SMITH. How fast did you go?

Mr. LIGHTOLLER. About 18 knots.

Senator SMITH. What was done when you reached Southampton?

Mr. LIGHTOLLER. The ship was heeled for stability.

Senator SMITH. Just describe that.

Mr. LIGHTOLLER. The builders knowing the exact weights on board, additional weights are placed on each side of the ship. A pendulum is suspended in the most convenient place in the ship with a plumb on the end of it, and a method of registering the difference with the plumb line; a number of men then transfer the weights from one side of the ship to the other, bringing all the weight on one side and transferring the whole of it back again; and with this, I believe the builders are able to draw up a stability scale.

Senator SMITH. From what part of the ship are these tests made?

Mr. LIGHTOLLER. The weights carried over, you mean?

Senator SMITH. Yes. From the upper part?

Mr. LIGHTOLLER. The "C" deck - the third deck down.

Senator SMITH. About the center of the ship?

Mr. LIGHTOLLER. Not quite the center of the ship.

Senator SMITH. Were there any tests made from the upper deck?

Mr. LIGHTOLLER. Not that I know of, sir.

Senator SMITH. What else was done at Southampton?

Mr. LIGHTOLLER. We shipped coal, provisions, cargo was taken on board, passed the Board of Trade tests and survey.

Senator SMITH. Did some British officer make the Board of Trade test?

Mr. LIGHTOLLER. The Southampton Board of Trade officer.

Senator SMITH. What did he do?

Mr. LIGHTOLLER. He carried out the requisite tests required by the Board of Trade.

Senator SMITH. Did you accompany him?

Mr. LIGHTOLLER. Yes; I was with him part of the time.

Senator SMITH. Who was this officer of the British Board of Trade?

Mr. LIGHTOLLER. Capt. Clark.

Senator SMITH. He was an officer?

Mr. LIGHTOLLER. He was purely a representative of the British Board of Trade, appointed by the British Board of Trade, with post at the port of Southampton; surveyor.

Senator SMITH. He was assigned to Southampton?

Mr. LIGHTOLLER. Yes, sir.

Senator SMITH. How old a man was he?

Mr. LIGHTOLLER. About 45.

Senator SMITH. Of English nationality?

Mr. LIGHTOLLER. Yes.

Senator SMITH. Had you ever seen him before?

Mr. LIGHTOLLER. Frequently.

Senator SMITH. Do you know whether he had any experience in marine service?

Mr. LIGHTOLLER. All surveyors, I understand, have been in command. I know he had for a number of years.

Senator SMITH. What does that mean - that he had been "in command"?

Mr. LIGHTOLLER. In command of a British ship; captain.

Senator SMITH. How much time did this officer spend on the ship?

Mr. LIGHTOLLER. That I could not say, sir.

Senator SMITH. How much did he spend when he was with you?

Mr. LIGHTOLLER. About four hours.

Senator SMITH. Then did you turn him over to some other officer?

Mr. LIGHTOLLER. Yes, sir.

Senator SMITH. To what other officer?

Mr. LIGHTOLLER. I think it was the first.

Senator SMITH. What is his name?

Mr. LIGHTOLLER. Mr. Murdoch.

Senator SMITH. Did he survive the Titanic disaster?

Mr. LIGHTOLLER. No, sir. He was chief then.

Senator SMITH. He did not survive?

Mr. LIGHTOLLER. No, sir.

Senator SMITH. Do you know whether any other officer of the ship accompanied this inspector during his stay on board?

Mr. LIGHTOLLER. That I could not say with certainty.

Senator SMITH. What is your best judgment about it?

Mr. LIGHTOLLER. I should say the marine superintendent was with him the whole time.

Senator SMITH. The marine superintendent?

Mr. LIGHTOLLER. Of the White Star Line, at Southampton.

Senator SMITH. What is his name?

Mr. LIGHTOLLER. Capt. Steele.

Senator SMITH. How old a man is he?

Mr. LIGHTOLLER. About 50.

Senator SMITH. Is he a commander?

Mr. LIGHTOLLER. Yes, sir.

Senator SMITH. Had you ever seen one of those ocean liners inspected by the British Board of Trade representative before?

Mr. LIGHTOLLER. Frequently.

Senator SMITH. How thorough are they about it?

Mr. LIGHTOLLER. Speaking of Capt. Clark, we call him a nuisance because he is so strict.

Senator SMITH. Capt. Clark?

Mr. LIGHTOLLER. Yes, sir.

Senator SMITH. Is he the marine officer?

Mr. LIGHTOLLER. That is the Board of Trade representative.

Senator SMITH. In what respect is he a nuisance?

Mr. LIGHTOLLER. Because he makes us fork out every detail.

106

Senator SMITH. I should suppose you would be quite willing to do that?

Mr. LIGHTOLLER. Perfectly willing.

Senator SMITH. Do you mean by that that he would call attention to the absence of tools, implements, and devices necessary for the ship's full equipment?

Mr. LIGHTOLLER. No, sir. He would insist upon them all being absolutely brought out on deck every time.

Senator SMITH. On what?

Mr. LIGHTOLLER. Everything that contributes to the ship's equipment.

Senator SMITH. What would that consist of?

Mr. LIGHTOLLER. The whole of the ship's life-saving equipment.

Senator SMITH. Life preservers?

Mr. LIGHTOLLER. Life preservers throughout the ship, all the boats turned out, uncovered, all the tanks examined, all the breakers examined, oars counted, boats turned out, rudders tried, all the davits tried - there was innumerable detail work.

Senator SMITH. And the boats lowered?

Mr. LIGHTOLLER. The boats lowered, put in the water, and pulled out, and brought back again, and if he was not satisfied, sent back again.

Senator SMITH: And the ropes and chains tested?

Mr. LIGHTOLLER. Yes, sir.

Senator SMITH: When he inspected your ship, about where would he find these life preservers?

Mr. LIGHTOLLER. Life belts in every room, in every compartment, where, as we say, there was habitation, where a man could live.

Senator SMITH. Would that include the steerage?

Mr. LIGHTOLLER. Yes, undoubtedly; and the crews quarters.

Senator SMITH. In the steerage do they have rooms?

Mr. LIGHTOLLER. Yes, sir.

Senator SMITH. Are they equipped?

Mr. LIGHTOLLER. Yes, sir.

Senator SMITH. With the same apparatus for the preservation of life with an emergency as the first and second cabins?

Mr. LIGHTOLLER. Identically the same.

Senator SMITH. You used the term "life belt."

Mr. LIGHTOLLER. Yes, sir.

Senator SMITH. I wish you would describe a life belt.

Mr. LIGHTOLLER. It consists of a series of pieces of cork - allow me to show you by illustration - a hole is cut in there [illustrating] for the head to go through and this falls over front and back, and there are tapes from the back then tied around the front. It is a new idea and very effective, because no one can make a mistake in putting it on.

Senator SMITH. Is there cork on both sides?

Mr. LIGHTOLLER. On both sides.

Senator SMITH. Are the arms free?

Mr. LIGHTOLLER. Free, absolutely.

Senator SMITH. And when in the water does this adhere or extend?

Mr. LIGHTOLLER. It is tied to the body.

Senator SMITH. It is tied to the body?

Mr. LIGHTOLLER. Yes, sir.

Senator SMITH. Have you ever had one of these on?

108

Mr. LIGHTOLLER. Yes, sir.

Senator SMITH. Have you ever been into the sea with one of them?

Mr. LIGHTOLLER. Yes, sir.

Senator SMITH. Where?

Mr. LIGHTOLLER. From the Titanic.

Senator SMITH. In this recent collision?

Mr. LIGHTOLLER. Yes, sir.

Senator SMITH. How long were you in the sea with a life belt on?

Mr. LIGHTOLLER. Between half an hour and an hour.

Senator SMITH. What time did you leave the ship?

Mr. LIGHTOLLER. I didn't leave it.

Senator SMITH. Did the ship leave you?

Mr. LIGHTOLLER. Yes, sir.

Senator SMITH. Did you stay until the ship had departed entirely?

Mr. LIGHTOLLER. Yes, sir.

Senator SMITH. I wish you would tell us whether the suction incidental to the sinking of this vessel was a great deterrent in making progress away from the boat?

Mr. LIGHTOLLER. It was hardly noticeable.

Senator SMITH. From what point on the vessel did you leave it?

Mr. LIGHTOLLER. On top of the officers' quarters.

Senator SMITH. And where were the officers' quarters?

Mr. LIGHTOLLER. Immediately abaft the bridge.

Senator SMITH. Immediately abaft the bridge?

Mr. LIGHTOLLER. Abaft the wheelhouse.

Senator SMITH. Was that pretty well toward the top of the vessel?

Mr. LIGHTOLLER. Yes, sir.

Senator SMITH. Were the lifeboats gone when you found yourself without any footing?

Mr. LIGHTOLLER. All except one.

Senator SMITH. Where was that one?

Mr. LIGHTOLLER. In the tackles, trying to get it over.

Senator SMITH. Did not the tackle work readily?

Mr. LIGHTOLLER. Yes, sir.

Senator SMITH. What delayed it?

Mr. LIGHTOLLER. It was the third boat over by the same tackles.

Senator SMITH. The third boat over by the same tackles?

Mr. LIGHTOLLER. Yes, sir.

Senator SMITH. From what deck?

Mr. LIGHTOLLER. The boat deck.

Senator SMITH. The sun deck?

Mr. LIGHTOLLER. The sun deck.

Senator SMITH. How close were you to this lifeboat at that time?

Mr. LIGHTOLLER. Fifteen feet.

Senator SMITH. Was it filled before starting to lower it?

Mr. LIGHTOLLER. It was not high enough to lower.

Senator SMITH. Why?

Mr. LIGHTOLLER. It was not high enough to lower. They were endeavoring to get it over the bulwarks, outboard; swinging it; getting it over the bulwarks. When it was over the bulwarks, then it would hang in the tackles, and until it hung in the tackles it was impossible to put anyone in it.

110

Senator SMITH. How far below the boat deck?

Mr. LIGHTOLLER. Above the boat deck.

Senator SMITH. How far above the boat deck?

Mr. LIGHTOLLER. About 4 feet 6 inches.

Senator SMITH. And it was lowered to the boat deck?

Mr. LIGHTOLLER. It did not get over the bulwarks to be lowered.

Senator SMITH. The last you saw of it?

Mr. LIGHTOLLER. Yes, sir.

Senator SMITH. Who was managing this tackle?

Mr. LIGHTOLLER. The first officer, Mr. Murdoch.

Senator SMITH. He lost his life?

Mr. LIGHTOLLER. Yes.

Senator SMITH. Did you see Mr. Ismay at that time?

Mr. LIGHTOLLER. No, sir.

Senator SMITH. Did you, at any time?

Mr. LIGHTOLLER. Yes, sir.

Senator SMITH. Where?

Mr. LIGHTOLLER. On the boat deck.

Senator SMITH. How long before she sunk?

Mr. LIGHTOLLER. At first, before we started the boats, when we started to uncover the boat.

Senator SMITH. I did not quite catch that.

Mr. LIGHTOLLER. When we started to uncover the boats.

Senator SMITH. How long was that after the collision?

Mr. LIGHTOLLER. About 20 minutes.

Senator SMITH. What was he doing?

Mr. LIGHTOLLER. Standing still.

Senator SMITH. Dressed?

Mr. LIGHTOLLER. I could not say, sir; it was too dark.

Senator SMITH. Was he talking to anyone?

Mr. LIGHTOLLER. No, sir.

Senator SMITH. He was alone?

Mr. LIGHTOLLER. Yes, sir.

Senator SMITH. On what deck?

Mr. LIGHTOLLER. On the boat deck.

Senator SMITH. Were there any other passengers on that deck?

Mr. LIGHTOLLER. Not that I saw at that time.

Senator SMITH. Did you see any there afterwards?

Mr. LIGHTOLLER. Plenty.

Senator SMITH. Had the passengers the right to go on the deck from below?

Mr. LIGHTOLLER. Every right.

Senator SMITH. There was no restraint at the staircase?

Mr. LIGHTOLLER. None.

Senator SMITH. Was that true as to the steerage?

Mr. LIGHTOLLER. The steerage have no right up there, sir.

Senator SMITH. Did they on that occasion?

Mr. LIGHTOLLER. Oh, yes.

Senator SMITH. There was no restraint?

Mr. LIGHTOLLER. Oh, absolutely none.

Senator SMITH. There must have been considerable confusion.

Mr. LIGHTOLLER. Not that I noticed.

Senator SMITH. Was everybody orderly?

Mr. LIGHTOLLER. Perfectly.

Senator SMITH. How long did you see Mr. Ismay there alone?

Mr. LIGHTOLLER. As I passed.

Senator SMITH. Where were you going at that time?

Mr. LIGHTOLLER. I was attending to the boats, seeing the men distributed, having the boat covers stripped off.

Senator SMITH. You say you were 15 feet from this last boat when it was lowered?

Mr. LIGHTOLLER. It was not lowered, sir. I was 15 feet from it when they were endeavoring to get it into the tackles.

Senator SMITH. Did you go nearer to it than that.

Mr. LIGHTOLLER. Did not have the opportunity, sir.

Senator SMITH. Why not?

Mr. LIGHTOLLER. The ship went down.

Senator SMITH. Was this boat ever lowered?

Mr. LIGHTOLLER. No, sir.

Senator SMITH. It remained in the tackle?

Mr. LIGHTOLLER. Yes, sir.

Senator SMITH. When did you see Mr. Ismay, with reference to the attempted lowering of this boat?

Mr. LIGHTOLLER. I saw Mr. Ismay, as I stated to you, sir.

Senator SMITH. Only once?

Mr. LIGHTOLLER. Yes, sir.

Senator SMITH. And that was about 20 minutes after the collision?

Mr. LIGHTOLLER. Yes, sir.

Senator SMITH. And there were no other passengers on that deck at that time?

Mr. LIGHTOLLER. Not that I noticed. I should notice Mr. Ismay naturally more than I should notice passengers.

Senator SMITH. Why?

Mr. LIGHTOLLER. Because I know him.

Senator SMITH. How long have you known him?

Mr. LIGHTOLLER. Since I have been in the company.

Senator SMITH. Are you quite well acquainted with the officers of this company?

Mr. LIGHTOLLER. I naturally know them by sight.

Senator SMITH. Does he know you?

Mr. LIGHTOLLER. Oh, he knew me; yes.

Senator SMITH. Did he speak to you?

Mr. LIGHTOLLER. No, sir.

Senator SMITH. Who was he with at that time?

Mr. LIGHTOLLER. No one.

Senator SMITH. Neither spoke to the other?

Mr. LIGHTOLLER. No, sir.

Senator SMITH. Did he see you?

Mr. LIGHTOLLER. Yes, sir. I don't know whether he recognized me.

Senator SMITH. Do you know where the captain was at that time?

Mr. LIGHTOLLER. I could not say, sir.

Senator SMITH. Did you see him on the bridge?

Mr. LIGHTOLLER. Previous to that I had seen him on the bridge.

Senator SMITH. How long before that?

Mr. LIGHTOLLER. About three minutes after the impact.

Senator SMITH. Did he leave the bridge or did he remain there and leave your point of occupation?

Mr. LIGHTOLLER. I left.

Senator SMITH. You left?

Mr. LIGHTOLLER. Yes, sir.

Senator SMITH. Where did you go?

Mr. LIGHTOLLER. Back to my berth.

Senator SMITH. What for?

Mr. LIGHTOLLER. There was no call for me to be on deck.

Senator SMITH. No call, or no cause?

Mr. LIGHTOLLER. As far as I could see, neither call nor cause.

Senator SMITH. You mean from the moment of the impact?

Mr. LIGHTOLLER. Yes, sir.

Senator SMITH. Did you believe the boat was in danger?

Mr. LIGHTOLLER. No, sir.

Senator SMITH. You felt that it was not a serious accident?

Mr. LIGHTOLLER. I did not think it was a serious accident

Senator SMITH. What was the force of the impact?

Mr. LIGHTOLLER. A slight jar and a grinding sound.

Senator SMITH. From front or side?

Mr. LIGHTOLLER. Well, naturally I should think it was in front, whether I could tell or not.

Senator SMITH. You could not tell exactly?

Mr. LIGHTOLLER. No, sir.

Senator SMITH. Was there a noise?

Mr. LIGHTOLLER. Very little.

Senator SMITH. Very little?

Mr. LIGHTOLLER. Very little.

Senator SMITH. Did you go back to your room under the impression that the boat had not been injured?

Mr. LIGHTOLLER. Yes, sir.

Senator SMITH. Didn't you tell Mr. Ismay that that night?

Mr. LIGHTOLLER. I had not seen Mr. Ismay then.

Senator SMITH. Did you tell him that afterwards?

Mr. LIGHTOLLER. Really, I could not say, sir.

Senator SMITH. Where were you when the impact occurred?

Mr. LIGHTOLLER. In my berth.

Senator SMITH. Asleep?

Mr. LIGHTOLLER. No, sir, I was just getting off asleep.

Senator SMITH. You arose?

Mr. LIGHTOLLER. Yes, sir.

Senator SMITH. Did you dress yourself?

Mr. LIGHTOLLER. No, sir.

Senator SMITH. What did you put on, if anything?

Mr. LIGHTOLLER. Nothing.

Senator SMITH. You went out of your room?

Mr. LIGHTOLLER. Yes, sir.

Senator SMITH. Forward?

Mr. LIGHTOLLER. Out on deck.

Senator SMITH. On deck?

Mr. LIGHTOLLER. Yes; I walked forward.

Senator SMITH. You walked forward how far?

Mr. LIGHTOLLER A matter of 10 feet, until I could see the bridge distinctly.

Senator SMITH. You could see the bridge distinctly; and the captain was on the bridge?

Mr. LIGHTOLLER. The captain and first officer.

Senator SMITH. Did you see any other officers at that time?

Mr. LIGHTOLLER. I did not notice them.

Senator SMITH. Had no alarm been given at that time?

Mr. LIGHTOLLER. None.

Senator SMITH. How much time elapsed after the impact and your appearance on the deck?

Mr. LIGHTOLLER. I should say about two or three minutes.

Senator SMITH. Two or three minutes?

Mr. LIGHTOLLER. Two minutes.

Senator SMITH. Then you returned? How long did you remain on deck?

Mr. LIGHTOLLER About two or three minutes.

Senator SMITH. At that time who else was on deck at that point?

Mr. LIGHTOLLER. Excluding the bridge, I saw no one except the third officer, who left his berth shortly after I did.

Senator SMITH. Did he join you?

Mr. LIGHTOLLER. Yes.

Senator SMITH. Did you confer about what had happened?

Mr. LIGHTOLLER. Yes, sir.

Senator SMITH. What did you conclude had happened?

Mr. LIGHTOLLER. Nothing much.

Senator SMITH. You knew there had been a collision?

Mr. LIGHTOLLER. Not necessarily a collision.

Senator SMITH. You knew you had struck something?

Mr. LIGHTOLLER. Yes, sir.

Senator SMITH. What did you assume it to be?

Mr. LIGHTOLLER. Ice.

Senator SMITH. Ice?

Mr. LIGHTOLLER. Yes, sir.

Senator SMITH. Why?

Mr. LIGHTOLLER. That was the conclusion one naturally jumps to around the Banks there.

Senator SMITH. Had you seen ice before?

Mr. LIGHTOLLER. No, sir.

Senator SMITH. Had there been any tests taken of the temperature of the water?

Mr. LIGHTOLLER. A test is taken of the water every two hours from the time the ship leaves until she returns to port.

Senator SMITH. Do you know whether these tests were made?

Mr. LIGHTOLLER. They were.

Senator SMITH. Did you make them?

Mr. LIGHTOLLER. Oh, no, sir.

Senator SMITH. Were they made under your direction?

Mr. LIGHTOLLER. No, sir.

Senator SMITH. How do you know they were made?

Mr. LIGHTOLLER. It is the routine of the ship.

Senator SMITH. You assume they were made?

Mr. LIGHTOLLER. Yes, sir.

Senator SMITH. But you can not say of your own knowledge that they were?

Mr. LIGHTOLLER. Not of my own actually seeing; no, sir.

Senator SMITH. How were these tests made?

Mr. LIGHTOLLER. By drawing water from over the side in a canvas bucket and placing a thermometer in it.

Senator SMITH. How far down did you dip this water, did you try to get surface water, or did you try to get below?

Mr. LIGHTOLLER. It is impossible to get water below; just the surface.

Senator SMITH. You get surface water entirely?

Mr. LIGHTOLLER. Yes, sir.

Senator SMITH. Those tests had been made that day?

Mr. LIGHTOLLER. Yes.

Senator SMITH. At intervals of two hours?

Mr. LIGHTOLLER. Yes, sir.

Senator SMITH. This was on Sunday?

Mr. LIGHTOLLER. Yes, sir.

Senator SMITH. Did you hear anything about the rope or chain or wire to which the test basins were attached not reaching the water at any time during those tests?

Mr. LIGHTOLLER. The bucket, you speak of?

Senator SMITH. Yes.

Mr. LIGHTOLLER. No, sir.

Senator SMITH. Would a complaint of that character come to you if it had been true?

Mr. LIGHTOLLER. Very quickly, I should think, sir.

Senator SMITH. How would it come to you?

Mr. LIGHTOLLER. From the person who saw it, I should think.

Senator SMITH. It would be his duty to report to you?

Mr. LIGHTOLLER. Undoubtedly.

Senator SMITH. Directly to you?

Mr. LIGHTOLLER. Directly to the officer in charge of the ship at the time.

Senator SMITH. Who was in charge of the ship on Sunday?

Mr. LIGHTOLLER. Each officer kept his own watch, sir.

Senator SMITH. Were you in charge?

Mr. LIGHTOLLER. During my watch.

Senator SMITH. What hours were your watch?

Mr. LIGHTOLLER. Six o'clock until 10 o'clock.

Senator SMITH. At night?

Mr. LIGHTOLLER. And morning.

Senator SMITH. So that from 6 o'clock in the evening on Sunday -

Mr. LIGHTOLLER. Yes, sir.

Senator SMITH. Until 10 o'clock you were in charge?

Mr. LIGHTOLLER. Yes, sir.

Senator SMITH. And during that time two tests should have been made of the temperature of the water for the purpose of ascertaining whether you were in the vicinity of icebergs?

Mr. LIGHTOLLER. No, sir.

Senator SMITH. For what purpose were the tests made?

Mr. LIGHTOLLER. They were routine, sir. It is customary to make them.

Senator SMITH. Do you mean that you take these tests when you are not in the vicinity of the Grand Banks?

Mr. LIGHTOLLER. From the time we leave port, any port in the world, until the time we get to the next port in any part of the world, these tests are taken by the White Star Line.

Senator SMITH. Did you take these tests when you are not in the vicinity of the Grand Banks?

Mr. LIGHTOLLER. We take them all the time; every two hours.

Senator SMITH. Regardless of location or circumstances?

Mr. LIGHTOLLER. Yes, sir.

Senator SMITH. Or conditions?

Mr. LIGHTOLLER. Yes, sir. I may except in narrow waters, such as rivers, or harbors. We do not take them here.

Senator SMITH. Is this test taken for the purpose of ascertaining the temperature of the water?

Mr. LIGHTOLLER. Yes, sir.

Senator SMITH. Merely?

Mr. LIGHTOLLER. Merely.

Senator SMITH. What does the temperature of the water indicate?

Mr. LIGHTOLLER. Nothing more than temperature of the air, sir.

Senator SMITH. Does it not indicate the proximity of a colder area or an unusual condition?

Mr. LIGHTOLLER. No, sir. It indicates cold water, sir, of course.

Senator SMITH. Can you tell us how cold that water was?

Mr. LIGHTOLLER. I know what it was when I was in it.

Senator SMITH. I should like to have your judgment about it.

Mr. LIGHTOLLER. I should say it was not much over freezing; how much, I could not say. It might be 33 or 34.

Senator SMITH. Not much over freezing?

Mr. LIGHTOLLER. No, sir.

Senator SMITH. What did the tests show?

Mr. LIGHTOLLER. I do not know, sir.

Senator SMITH. You mean they did not report to you?

Mr. LIGHTOLLER. It is entered in a book, sir.

Senator SMITH. And the fact, is not communicated to you directly after each test?

Mr. LIGHTOLLER. Not unless I ask for it.

Senator SMITH. And you did not think it necessary to ask for it that night?

Mr. LIGHTOLLER. No, sir.

Senator SMITH. You knew you were in the vicinity of icebergs; did you not?

Mr. LIGHTOLLER. Water is absolutely no guide to icebergs, sir.

Senator SMITH. I did not ask that. Did you know you were in the vicinity of icebergs?

Mr. LIGHTOLLER. No, sir.

Senator SMITH. Did you know of the wireless message from the Amerika to the Titanic, warning you that you were in the vicinity of icebergs?

Mr. LIGHTOLLER. From the Amerika to the Titanic?

Senator SMITH. Yes.

Mr. LIGHTOLLER. I can not say that I saw that individual message.

Senator SMITH. Did you hear of it?

Mr. LIGHTOLLER. I could not say, sir.

Senator SMITH. Would you have heard of it?

Mr. LIGHTOLLER. Most probably, sir.

Senator SMITH. If that had been the case?

Mr. LIGHTOLLER. Most probably, sir.

Senator SMITH. In fact, it would have been the duty of the person receiving this message to communicate it to you, for you were in charge of the ship?

Mr. LIGHTOLLER. Under the commander's orders, sir.

Senator SMITH. But you received no communication of that kind?

Mr. LIGHTOLLER. I do not know whether I received the Amerika's; I knew that a communication had come from some ship; I can not say that it was the Amerika.

Senator SMITH. Giving the latitude and the longitude of those icebergs?

Mr. LIGHTOLLER. No; no latitude.

Senator SMITH. And that they were prevalent?

Mr. LIGHTOLLER. Speaking of the icebergs and naming their longitude.

Senator SMITH. Just tell us, if anything, what did you hear about that, and from whom, if you can.

Mr. LIGHTOLLER. From what ship the message came I have forgotten; but the message contained information that there was ice from 49 to 51.

Senator SMITH. How do you know it came?

Mr. LIGHTOLLER. Because I saw it.

Senator SMITH. That is since the collision?

Mr. LIGHTOLLER. Not that I know of.

Senator SMITH. Have you seen it since the collision?

Mr. LIGHTOLLER. Not that I know of. Whether it was the same message or not. I have seen some. Whether it is the same or not, I do not know. I have not seen the same to my knowledge.

Senator SMITH. From whom did you get that information?

Mr. LIGHTOLLER. From the captain.

Senator SMITH. That night?

Mr. LIGHTOLLER. Yes.

Senator SMITH. At what time did you get that information?

Mr. LIGHTOLLER. I think it was that afternoon.

Senator SMITH. At what time?

Mr. LIGHTOLLER. About 1 o'clock.

Senator SMITH. Where were you then?

Mr. LIGHTOLLER. On the bridge.

Senator SMITH. With the captain?

Mr. LIGHTOLLER. Yes.

Senator SMITH. Where was the ship with reference to her latitude?

Mr. LIGHTOLLER. I could not tell you without working it out, sir.

Senator SMITH. What time was it in the day?

Mr. LIGHTOLLER. About 1 o'clock.

Senator SMITH. You were not then officer?

Mr. LIGHTOLLER. I was relieving for lunch.

Senator SMITH. So that from the time this communication came to you you were not in charge of the ship until 6 o'clock that night?

Mr. LIGHTOLLER. Exactly.

Senator SMITH. Who succeeded you as officer of the ship?

Mr. LIGHTOLLER. The first officer, Mr. Murdoch.

Senator SMITH. Did you communicate to him this information that the captain had given you on the bridge?

Mr. LIGHTOLLER. I communicated that when I was relieving him at 1 o'clock.

Senator SMITH. What did you tell him?

Mr. LIGHTOLLER. Exactly what was in the telegram.

Senator SMITH. What did he say?

Mr. LIGHTOLLER. "All right.".

Senator SMITH. So that the officers of the ship - the officer in charge, Mr. Murdoch, was fully advised by you that you were in proximity of these icebergs -

Mr. LIGHTOLLER. I would hardly call that proximity.

Senator SMITH. Pardon me and I will complete my question. And you were advised by the captain that that was the case. Or, reversing it, you were advised by the captain, and by word of mouth, and communicated that word to officer Murdoch, in charge of the ship, to which he replied, "All right"?

Mr. LIGHTOLLER. Yes, sir.

Senator SMITH. Did you hold any further consultation about it?

Mr. LIGHTOLLER. With the first officer? No, sir.

Senator SMITH. How fast was the boat going at that time?

Mr. LIGHTOLLER. About 21 or 22.

Senator SMITH. 21 or 22 knots?

Mr. LIGHTOLLER. Yes, sir.

Senator SMITH. Was that her maximum speed?

Mr. LIGHTOLLER. I do not know, sir. I could not say, sir.

Senator SMITH. Do you know whether she went any faster than that at any time on the trip?

Mr. LIGHTOLLER. As far as we understood she would eventually go faster than that when the ship was tuned up.

Senator SMITH. But that was as fast as she went on the trial tests.

Mr. LIGHTOLLER. I do not know what her speed was on the trial trip.

Senator SMITH. I thought you indicated it was about that. She was, however, running at her maximum speed at that time?

Mr. LIGHTOLLER. We understood she was not at her maximum speed.

Senator SMITH. That is, you understand that there was still reserve power there?

Mr. LIGHTOLLER. Yes.

Senator SMITH. That had not been exhausted?

Mr. LIGHTOLLER. Yes.

Senator SMITH. Did you have any instructions from anybody to exhaust that power?

Mr. LIGHTOLLER. None.

Senator SMITH. Did you have any ambition of your own to see it exhausted?

Mr. LIGHTOLLER. Yes, I dare say.

Senator SMITH. You wanted her to go as fast as she could?

Mr. LIGHTOLLER. At some time or other; yes.

Senator SMITH. Was that shared by your associates among the officers?

Mr. LIGHTOLLER. Oh, I could not say, sir.

Senator SMITH. Did they talk about it?

Mr. LIGHTOLLER. Naturally we talked; we wondered what her maximum speed would eventually be.

Senator SMITH. You were anxious to see it tested?

Mr. LIGHTOLLER. Not necessarily anxious.

Senator SMITH. Interested, however?

Mr. LIGHTOLLER. Interested; yes.

Senator SMITH. When you turned the ship over to the second officer, Mr. Murdoch -

Mr. LIGHTOLLER. The first officer.

Senator SMITH. When you turned the ship over to the first officer, Mr. Murdoch, where did you go?

Mr. LIGHTOLLER. What time are you speaking of now?

Senator SMITH. I am speaking of about noon or 1 o'clock.

Mr. LIGHTOLLER. I went to my lunch.

Senator SMITH. And what did you do after that?

Mr. LIGHTOLLER. I went below.

Senator SMITH. Where?

Mr. LIGHTOLLER. Below, to my berth or whatever it happened to be. We call the quarters generally below.

Senator SMITH. Did you find anybody there when you got below?

Mr. LIGHTOLLER. Yes. The watch below I suppose was there.

Senator SMITH. Did you have any talk with him about the word that the captain had given you?

Mr. LIGHTOLLER. No, sir.

Senator SMITH. Did you have any talk with anybody about it?

Mr. LIGHTOLLER. No, sir; not that I remember   .

Senator SMITH. How long did you remain in your room?

Mr. LIGHTOLLER. I dare say I was in and out of the room two or three times during the afternoon. Later on I laid down in the afternoon to sleep, and got up and wrote some letters, or something like that.

Senator SMITH. And took your place again in command of the ship, or rather, as officer of the watch, at 6 o'clock?

Mr. LIGHTOLLER. At 6 o'clock.

Senator SMITH. At that time did you say anything to the other officers who were on duty at the time about this information that the captain gave you?

Mr. LIGHTOLLER. Not that I remember, sir.

Senator SMITH. Was the lookout increased that evening after you took the watch?

Mr. LIGHTOLLER. No, sir.

Senator SMITH. What was the complement of your ship that night, in officers?

Mr. LIGHTOLLER. You mean on deck, sir?

Senator SMITH. Yes, sir.

Mr. LIGHTOLLER. Myself and two juniors.

Senator SMITH. Where were those two juniors stationed?

Mr. LIGHTOLLER. They have various duties to perform, taking the various parts of the ship; sometimes in the wheelhouse; at different periods one has to go the whole rounds of the ship and see that everything is in order.

Senator SMITH. When you came on watch at 6 o'clock, was the captain on the bridge, or did you see him?

Mr. LIGHTOLLER. I didn't see him at 6 o'clock.

Senator SMITH. When did you next see him?

Mr. LIGHTOLLER. About five minutes to 9 was the next time I saw him.

Senator SMITH. About five minutes to 9?

Mr. LIGHTOLLER. Yes, sir.

Senator SMITH. In his absence, who was on the bridge?

Mr. LIGHTOLLER. Myself.

Senator SMITH. Did you relieve him?

Mr. LIGHTOLLER. The captain?

Senator SMITH. Yes.

Mr. LIGHTOLLER. No, sir. The first officer. I beg your pardon; I relieved the chief.

Senator SMITH. You relieved the chief?

Mr. LIGHTOLLER. Yes, sir.

Senator SMITH. And went to the bridge?

Mr. LIGHTOLLER. I relieved the chief. The chief's watch was from 2 until 6. I relieved the chief officer at 6 o'clock and carried on the watch until 10.

Senator SMITH. Did you remain on the bridge?

Mr. LIGHTOLLER. Yes, sir.

Senator SMITH. From 6 until 10 o'clock?

Mr. LIGHTOLLER. Yes, sir.

Senator SMITH. During that time was each officer or man in his position in the forward part of the vessel?

Mr. LIGHTOLLER. Yes, sir.

Senator SMITH. Who was there, and where were they stationed?

Mr. LIGHTOLLER. Two men in the crow's nest, one man at the wheel, one man standing by.

Senator SMITH. What was the weather that night?

Mr. LIGHTOLLER. Clear and calm.

Senator SMITH. Were you at all apprehensive about your proximity to these icebergs?

Mr. LIGHTOLLER. No, sir.

Senator SMITH. And for that reason you did not think it necessary to increase the official lookout?

Mr. LIGHTOLLER. No, sir.

Senator SMITH. And that was not done?

Mr. LIGHTOLLER. No, sir.

Senator SMITH. From 6 until 10 o'clock was the captain on the bridge at all?

Mr. LIGHTOLLER. Yes, sir.

Senator SMITH. When did he arrive?

Mr. LIGHTOLLER. Five minutes to 9.

Senator SMITH. Five minutes to 9?

Mr. LIGHTOLLER. Yes, sir.

Senator SMITH. But he was not there from 6 o'clock until five minutes of 9?

Mr. LIGHTOLLER. I did not see him, sir.

Senator SMITH. You would have seen him if he had been there, would you not?

Mr. LIGHTOLLER. If he had been actually on the bridge, yes, I should have seen him.

Senator SMITH. You did not see him?

Mr. LIGHTOLLER. I did not see him.

Senator SMITH. And you were there during all that time?

Mr. LIGHTOLLER. During all that time.

Senator SMITH. When he came to the bridge at five minutes of 9 what did he say to you or what did you say to him? Who spoke first?

Mr. LIGHTOLLER. I could not say, sir. Probably one of us said "Good evening."

Senator SMITH. But you do not know who?

Mr. LIGHTOLLER. No.

Senator SMITH. Was anything else said?

Mr. LIGHTOLLER. Yes. We spoke about the weather; calmness of the sea; the clearness; about the time we should be getting up toward the vicinity of the ice and how we should recognize it if we should see it - freshening up our minds as to the indications that ice gives of its proximity. We just conferred together, generally, for 25 minutes.

Senator SMITH. For 20 or 25 minutes?

Mr. LIGHTOLLER. Yes, sir.

Senator SMITH. Was any reference made at that time to the wireless message from the Amerika?

Mr. LIGHTOLLER. Capt. Smith made a remark that if it was in a slight degree hazy there would be no doubt we should have to go very slowly.

Senator SMITH. Did you slow up?

Mr. LIGHTOLLER. That I do not know, sir.

Senator SMITH. You would have known if it had been done, would you not, during your watch?

Mr. LIGHTOLLER. Not necessarily so, sir.

Senator SMITH. Who would give the command?

Mr. LIGHTOLLER. The commander would send orders down to the chief engineer to reduce her by so many revolutions.

Senator SMITH. Through a megaphone?

Mr. LIGHTOLLER. No, sir; by word of hand.

Senator SMITH. By speaking tube?

Mr. LIGHTOLLER. No; by word of hand; notes.

Senator SMITH. Did you see anything of that kind done?

Mr. LIGHTOLLER. No, sir; I did not see it on the bridge.

Senator SMITH. And the captain was on the bridge?

Mr. LIGHTOLLER. Yes, sir.

Senator SMITH. How long did he remain on the bridge after coming there at 5 minutes of 9?

Mr. LIGHTOLLER. He remained there until about 20 minutes past 9, or something like that.

Senator SMITH. About 20 minutes past 9?

Mr. LIGHTOLLER. About 25 minutes altogether.

Senator SMITH. Then did he leave the bridge?

Mr. LIGHTOLLER. He left the bridge.

Senator SMITH. With any special injunction upon you?

Mr. LIGHTOLLER. Yes, sir.

Senator SMITH. What did he say?

Mr. LIGHTOLLER. "If in the slightest degree doubtful, let me know."

Senator SMITH. What did you say to him?

Mr. LIGHTOLLER. "All right, sir."

Senator SMITH. You kept the ship on its course?

Mr. LIGHTOLLER. Yes, sir.

Senator SMITH. And at about the same speed?

Mr. LIGHTOLLER. Yes, sir; as far as I know.

Senator SMITH. When did you next see the captain?

Mr. LIGHTOLLER. When I came out of the quarters, after the impact.

Senator SMITH. You mean that he did not return to the bridge until your watch expired?

Mr. LIGHTOLLER. No, sir.

Senator SMITH. About 10 o'clock?

Mr. LIGHTOLLER. Yes, sir.

Senator SMITH. You left?

Mr. LIGHTOLLER. Yes, sir.

Senator SMITH. And Murdoch took command?

Mr. LIGHTOLLER. Yes, sir.

Senator SMITH. Do you know where you were at the hour that you turned over the watch to Mr. Murdoch?

Mr. LIGHTOLLER. Not now, sir.

Senator SMITH. Did you know at the time?

Mr. LIGHTOLLER. Yes, sir.

Senator SMITH. Can you give us any idea?

Mr. LIGHTOLLER. When I ended the watch we roughly judged that we should be getting toward the vicinity of the ice, as reported by that Marconigram that I saw, somewhere about 11 o'clock.

Senator SMITH. That you would be in that latitude?

Mr. LIGHTOLLER. Longitude

Senator SMITH. At 11 o'clock.

Mr. LIGHTOLLER. Somewhere about 11; yes.

Senator SMITH. Did you talk with Mr. Murdoch about that phase of it when you left the watch?

Mr. LIGHTOLLER. About what?

Senator SMITH. I say, did you talk with Mr. Murdoch about the iceberg situation when you left the watch?

Mr. LIGHTOLLER. No, sir.

Senator SMITH. Did he ask you anything about it?

Mr. LIGHTOLLER. No, sir.

Senator SMITH. What was said between you?

Mr. LIGHTOLLER. We remarked on the weather, about its being calm, clear. We remarked the distance we could see. We seemed to be able to see a long distance. Everything was very clear. We could see the stars setting down to the horizon.

Senator SMITH. It was cold, was it not?

Mr. LIGHTOLLER. Yes, sir.

Senator SMITH. Sharp?

Mr. LIGHTOLLER. Yes, sir.

Senator SMITH. How cold was it?

Mr. LIGHTOLLER. Thirty-one, sir.

Senator SMITH. Above zero?

Mr. LIGHTOLLER. Thirty-one degrees above zero, yes, sir.

Senator SMITH. Is that unusually cold for that longitude?

Mr. LIGHTOLLER. No, sir.

Senator SMITH. At that time of the year?

Mr. LIGHTOLLER. No, sir.

Senator SMITH. Did you see Mr. Murdoch after that?

Mr. LIGHTOLLER. Yes, sir; I saw him when I came out of the quarters after the impact.

Senator SMITH. Where was he?

Mr. LIGHTOLLER. On the bridge.

Senator SMITH. With the captain?

Mr. LIGHTOLLER. One on one side, and one on the other side of the bridge; one on each side.

Senator SMITH. Did you speak to him after that?

Mr. LIGHTOLLER. No, sir.

Senator SMITH. I mean after he took the watch?

Mr. LIGHTOLLER. No, sir.

Senator SMITH. You never spoke to him again?

Mr. LIGHTOLLER. No; sir.

Senator SMITH. You were not together when finally parted from the ship?

Mr. LIGHTOLLER. No, sir.

Senator SMITH. You saw him on the bridge at the time?

Mr. LIGHTOLLER. Immediately after the impact; yes, sir.

Senator SMITH. Did he remain there until the end?

Mr. LIGHTOLLER. He was getting the boats out on the starboard side later on.

Senator SMITH. Later?

Mr. LIGHTOLLER. Yes, sir.

Senator SMITH. Did you see him at that work?

Mr. LIGHTOLLER. No, sir; I was on the port side.

Senator SMITH. How do you know that he did it?

Mr. LIGHTOLLER. I saw him at the last boat.

Senator SMITH. Just what time he left the bridge, I don't suppose you know?

Mr. LIGHTOLLER. No, sir.

Senator SMITH. Where did you last see the captain?

Mr. LIGHTOLLER. On the boat deck, sir.

Senator SMITH. On the boat deck?

Mr. LIGHTOLLER. Yes, sir.

Senator SMITH. How long before the vessel sank?

Mr. LIGHTOLLER. I could not say, sir; I saw him about the boat deck two or three times. I had no occasion to go to him.

Senator SMITH. Was the vessel broken in two in any manner, or intact?

Mr. LIGHTOLLER. Absolutely intact.

Senator SMITH. On the decks?

Mr. LIGHTOLLER. Intact, sir.

Senator SMITH. When you came out of your room after the impact, did you see any ice on the decks?

Mr. LIGHTOLLER. No, sir.

Senator SMITH. Did you see or hear any exclamations of pain?

Mr. LIGHTOLLER. No, sir.

Senator SMITH. Do you know whether anyone was injured?

Mr. LIGHTOLLER. No, sir.

Senator SMITH. By ice on deck?

Mr. LIGHTOLLER. No, sir.

Senator SMITH. Tell us, as nearly as you can, just where you saw the captain last, with reference to the sinking of this ship.

Mr. LIGHTOLLER. I think the bridge was the last place I saw him, sir; I am not sure. I think he was crossing the bridge.

Senator SMITH. What do you mean by that?

Mr. LIGHTOLLER. Walking across.

Senator SMITH. From one side to the other?

Mr. LIGHTOLLER. No, sir; just coming across. I merely recognized a glimpse. I have a slight recollection of having seen him whilst I was walking. It is my recollection that I saw him crossing the bridge. I think that was the last.

Senator SMITH. How large was this bridge? How large was it on the Titanic?

Mr. LIGHTOLLER. It extends the width of the ship, sir.

Senator SMITH. It extend the width of the ship?

Mr. LIGHTOLLER. Yes, sir; and 18 inches over each side.

Senator SMITH. And how far forward?

Mr. LIGHTOLLER. In amidships, about 20 feet; in the wings, about 10 feet.

Senator SMITH. When you saw him was he giving any orders?

Mr. LIGHTOLLER. I was not near enough to know, sir.

Senator SMITH. How near were you?

Mr. LIGHTOLLER. About 50 feet away.

Senator SMITH. What did he seem to be doing - pacing?

Mr. LIGHTOLLER. No, sir; not pacing. Just walking straight across, as if he had some object that he was walking toward.

Senator SMITH. He was walking from one side to the other?

Mr. LIGHTOLLER. Yes, sir; from starboard to port.

Senator SMITH. Did that give him a full sweep of view of the situation?

Mr. LIGHTOLLER. Yes, sir.

Senator SMITH. If he had been giving orders would you have heard them?

Mr. LIGHTOLLER. Yes, sir.

Senator SMITH. And you did not hear any such thing at that time?

Mr. LIGHTOLLER. At that time; no, sir.

Senator SMITH. What were the last orders you heard him give?

Mr. LIGHTOLLER. When I asked him, "Shall I put the women and children in the boats?" he replied, "Yes; and lower away." Those were the last orders he gave.

Senator SMITH. Where was he at that time?

Mr. LIGHTOLLER. About abreast the No. 6 boat.

Senator SMITH. How long was that before the ship sunk?

Mr. LIGHTOLLER. Approximately somewhere about a quarter to 1, say. I don't know what time it was, sir. It would be only a guess.

Senator SMITH. It was after this impact?

Mr. LIGHTOLLER. Yes, sir.

Senator SMITH. After the collision?

Mr. LIGHTOLLER. Yes, sir.

Senator SMITH. And about how long after? What time did the collision occur?

Mr. LIGHTOLLER. I do not know. I understand - I only gather it - that it occurred shortly before 12 o'clock.

Senator SMITH. When you heard it, did you look at your watch or make a note of it?

Mr. LIGHTOLLER. No, sir.

Senator SMITH. How long was the vessel afloat after this collision?

Mr. LIGHTOLLER. That I do not know either, only from what I was told.

Senator SMITH. What were you told?

Mr. LIGHTOLLER. I was told she sunk at 2:20.

Senator SMITH. Who told you that?

Mr. LIGHTOLLER. We came to the conclusion amongst the officers, by various indications.

Senator SMITH. Did any officer that you communicated with know the exact moment of this impact or collision?

Mr. LIGHTOLLER. That I could not say, sir.

Senator SMITH. Of course you had a watch with you?

Mr. LIGHTOLLER. No, sir.

Senator SMITH. Did you have a watch in your room?

Mr. LIGHTOLLER. In my room; yes, sir.

Senator SMITH. Did you keep it or is it gone?

Mr. LIGHTOLLER. Oh, it is gone, sir.

Senator SMITH. You did not know whether it was running or stopped? You did not look at it?

Mr. LIGHTOLLER. I did not look at it, sir.

Senator SMITH. You asked the captain on the boat deck whether the lifeboats should take the women and children first, if I understand you correctly?

Mr. LIGHTOLLER. Not quite, sir; I asked him: "Shall I put the women and children in the boats?" The captain replied, "Yes, and lower away."

Senator SMITH. What did you then do?

Mr. LIGHTOLLER. I carried out his orders.

Senator SMITH. Except as to this one boat that could not be lowered?

Mr. LIGHTOLLER. I am speaking of the port side of the ship. I was running the port side only.

Senator SMITH. Were all the boats lowered on the port side?

Mr. LIGHTOLLER. They were all lowered with the exception of one, the last boat, which was stowed on top of the officers' quarters. We had not time to launch it nor yet to open it.

Senator SMITH. I did not get the first word, Was it injured?

Mr. LIGHTOLLER. No, sir; I said it was stowed on top of the officers' quarters. And when all the other boats were carried away, I called for the men to go up there, told them to cut her adrift and throw her down.

Senator SMITH. How did it happen to be stowed up there? Was that an unusual place for it?

Mr. LIGHTOLLER. No, sir.

Senator SMITH. Well, what happened to that boat?

Mr. LIGHTOLLER. It floated off the ship, sir.

Senator SMITH. It floated off?

Mr. LIGHTOLLER. Yes.

Senator SMITH. Without anyone in it?

Mr. LIGHTOLLER. I understand the men standing on top, who assisted to launch it down, jumped onto it as it was on the deck and floated off with it.

Senator SMITH. What type of boat was it?

Mr. LIGHTOLLER. Collapsible.

Senator SMITH. Did you see it afterwards?

Mr. LIGHTOLLER. Eventually. It was the boat that I got on.

Senator SMITH. Eventually that was the boat that you got on?

Mr. LIGHTOLLER. Yes, sir; bottom up.

Senator SMITH. Did you see the captain after that final order with reference to the women and children?

Mr. LIGHTOLLER. Yes, sir.

Senator SMITH. Where?

Mr. LIGHTOLLER. Walking across the bridge, sir.

Senator SMITH. Did you have any further communication with him?

Mr. LIGHTOLLER. No, sir; none.

Senator SMITH. So far as you know, was that the last place that he was seen?

Mr. LIGHTOLLER. I could not say, sir.

Senator SMITH. You don't know what occurred to the captain after that?

Mr. LIGHTOLLER. No, sir.

Senator SMITH. This lifeboat which was taken from the top of the officers' quarters, and that you finally reached, contained how many people?

Mr. LIGHTOLLER. When it floated off the ship?

Senator SMITH. Yes.

Mr. LIGHTOLLER. I could not say how many.

Senator SMITH. How many after you had gotten into it?

Mr. LIGHTOLLER. We were thrown off a couple of times. It was cleared; it was a flat collapsible boat. When I came to it, it was bottom up, and there was no one on it.

Senator SMITH. No one on it?

Mr. LIGHTOLLER. And it was on the other side of the ship.

Senator SMITH. What did you do when you came to it?

Mr. LIGHTOLLER. I hung on to it.

Senator SMITH. You floated with it merely?

Mr. LIGHTOLLER. Yes, sir.

Senator SMITH. Was that all the service it ever rendered? Was that the only service this lifeboat performed?

Mr. LIGHTOLLER. No, sir. Eventually about 30 of us got in it.

Senator SMITH. Tell us just how it occurred.

Mr. LIGHTOLLER. From the time the ship went down you mean?

Senator SMITH. No; from the time you found this over-turned lifeboat.

Mr. LIGHTOLLER. Yes, sir. Immediately after finding that overturned lifeboat, and when I came up alongside of it, there were quite a lot of us in the water around it preparatory to getting up on it.

Senator SMITH. With life preservers?

Mr. LIGHTOLLER. Yes, sir. Then the forward funnel fell down

Senator SMITH. Were there any persons there without life preservers?

Mr. LIGHTOLLER. No, sir. Not that I know of. The forward funnel falling down, it fell alongside of the lifeboat, about 4 inches clear of it.

Senator SMITH. What was this that fell?

Mr. LIGHTOLLER. The forward funnel.

Senator SMITH. Did it strike the boat?

Mr. LIGHTOLLER. It missed the boat.

Senator SMITH. Then what?

Mr. LIGHTOLLER. It fell on all the people there were alongside of the boat, if there were any there.

Senator SMITH. Injure any of them seriously?

Mr. LIGHTOLLER. I could not say, sir.

Senator SMITH. Did it kill anybody?

Mr. LIGHTOLLER. I could not say, sir.

Senator SMITH. Was this vessel sinking pretty rapidly at that time?

Mr. LIGHTOLLER. Pretty quickly, sir.

Senator SMITH. Do you know any of the men who were in the water as you were and who boarded this lifeboat?

Mr. LIGHTOLLER. Yes, sir.

Senator SMITH. Give their names.

Mr. LIGHTOLLER. Mr. Thayer, a first-class passenger; the second Marconi operator - I can tell you his name in a minute - Bride.

Senator SMITH. Was that the boat that Col. Gracie -

Mr. LIGHTOLLER. Oh, yes; and Col. Gracie.

Senator SMITH. Col. Gracie of the United States Army?

Mr. LIGHTOLLER. I think I have his card.

Senator SMITH. It was Col. Gracie, anyway?

Mr. LIGHTOLLER. Col. Gracie was on the upturned boat with me; yes.

Senator SMITH. Was he on the upturned boat before you got it righted around?

Mr. LIGHTOLLER. We never righted it.

Senator SMITH. You never righted it?

Mr. LIGHTOLLER. No, sir, we could not.

Senator SMITH. Who else was there?

Mr. LIGHTOLLER. I think all the rest were firemen taken out of the water, sir. Those are the only passengers that I know of.

Senator SMITH. No other passengers?

Mr. LIGHTOLLER. There were two or three that died. I think there were three or four who died during the night.

142

Senator SMITH. Aboard this boat with you?

Mr. LIGHTOLLER. Yes, sir; I think the senior Marconi operator was on the boat and died. The Marconi junior operator told me that the senior was on this boat and died.

Senator SMITH. From the cold?

Mr. LIGHTOLLER. Presumably.

Senator SMITH. Not from the blow of this -

Mr. LIGHTOLLER. No; not that I know of.

Senator SMITH. How many persons altogether?

Mr. LIGHTOLLER. I should roughly estimate about 30. She was packed standing from stem to stern at daylight.

Senator SMITH. Was there any effort made by others to board her?

Mr. LIGHTOLLER. We took all on board that we could.

Senator SMITH. I understand, but I wanted to know whether there was any effort made by others to get aboard?

Mr. LIGHTOLLER. Not that I saw.

Senator SMITH. There must have been a great number of people in the water?

Mr. LIGHTOLLER. But not near us. They were some distance away from us.

Senator SMITH. How far?

Mr. LIGHTOLLER. It seemed about a half a mile.

Senator SMITH. Was not this the only raft or craft in sight?

Mr. LIGHTOLLER. It was dark, sir.

Senator SMITH. Yes. But this was the only thing there was to get on at that time?

Mr. LIGHTOLLER. With the exception of the wreckage.

Senator SMITH. With the exception of what floated off the ship?

Mr. LIGHTOLLER. Yes, sir.

Senator SMITH. In the form of wreckage?

Mr. LIGHTOLLER. Yes, sir.

Senator SMITH. Did you see Col. Gracie?

Mr. LIGHTOLLER. I don't know whether I saw him, sir. I met him on the Carpathia afterwards, of course.

Senator SMITH. Do you remember seeing him in the water?

Mr. LIGHTOLLER. No, sir.

Senator SMITH. Who took command of that overturned lifeboat?

Mr. LIGHTOLLER. I did, as far as command was necessary.

Senator SMITH. Did your judgement rule the conduct of those on it?

Mr. LIGHTOLLER. Yes, sir; that is my reason for saying that I believe it was mostly the crew of the ship, because of the implicit obedience.

Senator SMITH. When you left the ship, did you see any women or children on board?

Mr. LIGHTOLLER. None whatever.

Senator SMITH. Could you give us any estimate whatever as to the number of first and second class passengers that were on board when the ship went down?

Mr. LIGHTOLLER. No, sir.

Senator SMITH. Were there any on the so-called boat deck?

Mr. LIGHTOLLER. Yes, sir.

Senator SMITH. Were there quite a number, in your opinion?

Mr. LIGHTOLLER A number of people - what they were, first, second, or third, crew or firemen, I could not say, sir.

Senator SMITH. But there were many people still on the ship?

Mr. LIGHTOLLER. Yes, sir.

Senator SMITH. And, so far as you could observe, could you tell whether they were equipped with life preservers?

Mr. LIGHTOLLER. As far as I could see, throughout the whole of the passengers, or the whole of the crew, everyone was equipped with a life preserver, for I looked for it especially.

Senator SMITH. Were the passengers on those decks instructed at any time to go to one side or the other of the ship?

Mr. LIGHTOLLER. Yes.

Senator SMITH. What do you know about that?

Mr. LIGHTOLLER. When the ship was taking a heavy list - not a heavy list - but she was taking a list over to port, the order was called, I think, by the chief officer. "Everyone on the starboard side to straighten her up," which I repeated.

Senator SMITH. How long before you left the ship?

Mr. LIGHTOLLER. I could not say, sir.

Senator SMITH. About how long?

Mr. LIGHTOLLER. Half an hour or three quarters of an hour.

Senator SMITH. Before you left?

Mr. LIGHTOLLER. Yes.

Senator SMITH. How were these passengers selected in going to the lifeboats?

Mr. LIGHTOLLER. By their sex.

Senator SMITH. Whenever you saw a woman?

Mr. LIGHTOLLER. Precisely.

Senator SMITH. She was invited to go into one of these boats?

Mr. LIGHTOLLER. Excepting the stewardesses. We turned several of those away.

Senator SMITH. Except the employees?

Mr. LIGHTOLLER. Except the stewardesses; yes.

Senator SMITH. And did you see any attempt made to get women to enter the lifeboats who refused to go?

Mr. LIGHTOLLER. Yes, sir.

Senator SMITH. How many?

Mr. LIGHTOLLER. I couldn't say, sir.

Senator SMITH. Several?

Mr. LIGHTOLLER. A few.

Senator SMITH. What reason was given why they did not?

Mr. LIGHTOLLER. I had not time; I didn't notice. Merely they would not come.

Senator SMITH. Did they ask that their families be taken?

Mr. LIGHTOLLER. Yes; one or two.

Senator SMITH. And were families taken, to your knowledge?

Mr. LIGHTOLLER. Not to my knowledge.

Senator SMITH. Were the boat that was on top of the officers' quarters that overturned, and the boat that was stuck in the tackle both made use of in any way, or but one?

Mr. LIGHTOLLER. But one.

Senator SMITH. So that altogether there were how many lifeboats actually used?

Mr. LIGHTOLLER. Nineteen.

Senator SMITH. How many actually picked up by the Carpathia?

Mr. LIGHTOLLER.   All accounted for.

Senator SMITH.   One, however, was badly injured, and another lifeboat took the passengers from it, did they not?

Mr. LIGHTOLLER.   That was the upturned one that I was on.

Senator SMITH.   That was the upturned one that you were on?

Mr. LIGHTOLLER.   Yes, sir.

Senator SMITH.   And they took you into another lifeboat?

Mr. LIGHTOLLER.   Yes, sir.

Senator SMITH.   All of those who were with you?

Mr. LIGHTOLLER.   Yes, sir.

Senator SMITH.   Was the lifeboat full at that time?

Mr. LIGHTOLLER.   I counted 65 heads, not including myself or any that were in the bottom of the boat. I roughly estimated about 75 in the boat.

Senator SMITH.   Was the boat safe with that number of people in it?

Mr. LIGHTOLLER.   Safe in smooth water only.

Senator SMITH.   How many of those lifeboats did you help load?

Mr. LIGHTOLLER.   All except one or two on the port side.

Senator SMITH.   Who determined the number of people who should go into the lifeboats?

Mr. LIGHTOLLER.   I did.

Senator SMITH.   How did you reach a conclusion as to the number that should be permitted to go in?

Mr. LIGHTOLLER.   My own judgment about the strength of the tackle.

Senator SMITH. How many did you put in each boat?

Mr. LIGHTOLLER. In the first boat I put about 20 or 25. Twenty, sir.

Senator SMITH. How many men?

Mr. LIGHTOLLER. No men.

Senator SMITH. How many seamen?

Mr. LIGHTOLLER. Two.

Senator SMITH. In the first boat?

Mr. LIGHTOLLER. Yes, sir.

Senator SMITH. Was that sufficient to take care of the boat?

Mr. LIGHTOLLER. We wanted them up on deck.

Senator SMITH. For what purpose?

Mr. LIGHTOLLER. Lowering away the boats.

Senator SMITH. Do you mean that there would not have been sufficient on deck and to man the lifeboats at the same time?

Mr. LIGHTOLLER. Not to distribute more than two to a boat, sir. It would not be safe.

Senator SMITH. That is not the usual requirement, is it - two to a boat?

Mr. LIGHTOLLER. Quite sufficient under the conditions.

Senator SMITH. As a matter of fact, women were obliged to row those boats for hours?

Mr. LIGHTOLLER. Yes, a great many did, I know.

Senator SMITH. That indicated that they were not fully equipped?

Mr. LIGHTOLLER. Not necessarily, sir.

Senator SMITH. How many oars in a boat?

Mr. LIGHTOLLER. I think it is 16, the full equipment.

148

Senator SMITH. How many persons can use an oar at one time? I do not mean how many can, but I mean how many ordinarily would?

Mr. LIGHTOLLER. Do you mean during boat practice, for instance?

Senator SMITH. I should like to know how many during practice and I should like to know how many in actual danger such as this.

Mr. LIGHTOLLER. We would man about five oars a side. In the boat I was in we could pull only three oars.

Senator SMITH. You couldn't pull at all, could you, in your boat?

Mr. LIGHTOLLER. We managed to keep our head to the sea with three oars.

Senator SMITH. You mean you got hold of three oars after this boat was turned over?

Mr. LIGHTOLLER. No, sir. The one that picked us up, afterwards.

Senator SMITH. You did not have any means of propelling your craft until you were taken from this up-turned boat?

Mr. LIGHTOLLER. A couple of bits of wood we picked up, only.

Senator SMITH. You say five men on a side?

Mr. LIGHTOLLER. As far as I remember, five a side.

Senator SMITH. Does that mean that a single individual will be at an oar?

Mr. LIGHTOLLER. Not necessarily. You can do what we call double or treble bank.

Senator SMITH. Tell me what that is.

Mr. LIGHTOLLER. Two or three pulling abreast of one another, one holding an oar here, another there, and another one there.

Senator SMITH. Abreast?

Mr. LIGHTOLLER. Abreast, another couple in front turned around facing and pushing the oar.

Senator SMITH. Pushing?

Mr. LIGHTOLLER. Pushing, standing up in the boat.

Senator SMITH. So that it is entirely possible and often the case that men face one another in working these oars?

Mr. LIGHTOLLER. Precisely.

Senator SMITH. And therefore, in the case of a boat with its full complement of men, one man might be where he could see the ship, pulling with his back to the sea and another with his back to the ship and his face to the sea?

Mr. LIGHTOLLER. Precisely.

Senator SMITH. You say there were about 25 in this first lifeboat?

Mr. LIGHTOLLER. About that.

Senator SMITH. And that it was loaded under your orders?

Mr. LIGHTOLLER. Under my orders.

Senator SMITH. What happened to that lifeboat, the first one loaded?

Mr. LIGHTOLLER. It was loaded and sent away from the ship.

Senator SMITH. Did it not return to the ship because it was only half loaded?

Mr. LIGHTOLLER. Not to my knowledge, sir.

Senator SMITH. As a matter of fact it was not much more than half loaded, was it?

Mr. LIGHTOLLER. You mean its floating capacity?

Senator SMITH. Yes.

Mr. LIGHTOLLER. Floating capacity; no.

Senator SMITH. How did it happen you did not put more people into that boat?

Mr. LIGHTOLLER. Because I did not consider it safe.

Senator SMITH. In a great emergency like that, where there were limited facilities, could you not have afforded to try to put more people into that boat?

Mr. LIGHTOLLER. I did not know it was urgent then. I had no idea it was urgent.

Senator SMITH. You did not know it was urgent.

Mr. LIGHTOLLER. Nothing like it.

Senator SMITH. Supposing you had known it was urgent, what would you have done?

Mr. LIGHTOLLER I would have acted to the best of my judgment then.

Senator SMITH. Tell me what you would have thought wise.

Mr. LIGHTOLLER. I would have taken more risks. I should not have considered it wise to put more in, but I might have taken risks.

Senator SMITH. As a matter of fact are not these lifeboats so constructed as to accommodate 40 people?

Mr. LIGHTOLLER. Sixty-five in the water, sir.

Senator SMITH. Sixty-five in the water, and about 40 as they are being put into the water?

Mr. LIGHTOLLER. No, sir.

Senator SMITH. How?

Mr. LIGHTOLLER. No, sir; it all depends on your gears, sir. If it were an old ship, you would barely dare to put 25 in.

Senator SMITH. But this was a new one?

Mr. LIGHTOLLER. And therefore I took chances with her afterwards.

Senator SMITH. You put 25 in?

Mr. LIGHTOLLER. In the first.

Senator SMITH. And two men?

Mr. LIGHTOLLER. And two men.

Senator SMITH. How were those two men selected; arbitrarily by you?

Mr. LIGHTOLLER. No, sir. They were selected by me; yes.

Senator SMITH. Who were they?

Mr. LIGHTOLLER. I could not say, sir.

Senator SMITH. How did you happen to choose those particular men?

Mr. LIGHTOLLER. Because they were standing near.

Senator SMITH. Did they want to go?

Mr. LIGHTOLLER. I did not ask them.

Senator SMITH. You did not call for volunteers?

Mr. LIGHTOLLER. They went by my orders.

Senator SMITH. You directed that it should be done?

Mr. LIGHTOLLER. Yes.

Senator SMITH. And they got in?

Mr. LIGHTOLLER. They did.

Senator SMITH. And 23 people besides?

Mr. LIGHTOLLER. I should say about 24; something like that.

Senator SMITH. Did you see any lifeboat return to the ship and take on additional passengers?

Mr. LIGHTOLLER. No, sir.

Senator SMITH. How many did the second boat contain?

Mr. LIGHTOLLER. About 30.

Senator SMITH. How many men?

Mr. LIGHTOLLER. Two.

Senator SMITH. How many women and children?

Mr. LIGHTOLLER. About 30.

Senator SMITH. Women or women and children?

Mr. LIGHTOLLER. I should say, roughly 30, and probably grown ups.

Senator SMITH. What side were you loading on?

Mr. LIGHTOLLER. On the port side of the ship, sir.

Senator SMITH. Were those 30 lowered?

Mr. LIGHTOLLER. Yes; lowered and sent away.

Senator SMITH. From what deck?

Mr. LIGHTOLLER. From the boat deck.

Senator SMITH. You do not know, I suppose, whether they were first or second cabin passengers?

Mr. LIGHTOLLER. No.

Senator SMITH. There were two men?

Mr. LIGHTOLLER. Two men, as far as I remember, sir.

Senator SMITH. Did you see that boat again alongside or any place else?

Mr. LIGHTOLLER. By the Titanic, sir?

Senator SMITH. Yes.

Mr. LIGHTOLLER. No; not to my knowledge.

Senator SMITH. How many did the third boat contain?

Mr. LIGHTOLLER. By the time I came to the third boat I was aware that it was getting serious, and then I started to take chances.

Senator SMITH. How long did it take to lower a boat - fill it and lower it?

Mr. LIGHTOLLER. Just filling it and lowering it, and not clearing away?

Senator SMITH. Filling and lowering and clearing?

Mr. LIGHTOLLER. We clear it away first then heave it out over the side, then lower it down level with the rail, and then commence to fill it with people. Previous to that we have to take the covers all off, haul out all the falls and coil them down clear.

Senator SMITH. How long do you think it took you to uncover and lower that lifeboat?

Mr. LIGHTOLLER. It is difficult to say, sir; 15 or 20 minutes.

Senator SMITH. Were there any lifeboats being lowered from the other side at the same time?

Mr. LIGHTOLLER. I do not know, sir.

Senator SMITH. How did it happen that you had charge of that feature?

Mr. LIGHTOLLER. Because I took charge.

Senator SMITH. You took charge of it?

Mr. LIGHTOLLER. Yes, sir.

Senator SMITH. And where was Mr. Murdoch at that time?

Mr. LIGHTOLLER. As far as I know, he had charge of the starboard side.

Senator SMITH. How many passengers did the third boat contain?

Mr. LIGHTOLLER. I can only guess. I filled her up as full as I could, and lowered her as full as I dared.

Senator SMITH. How many seamen?

Mr. LIGHTOLLER. Two.

Senator SMITH. You followed that rule?

Mr. LIGHTOLLER. I followed that rule throughout.

Senator SMITH. You filled it full?

Mr. LIGHTOLLER. As full as I possibly dared.

Senator SMITH. Did you have any difficulty in doing it?

Mr. LIGHTOLLER. In what manner?

Senator SMITH. Were the people ready to go?

Mr. LIGHTOLLER. Perfectly quiet and ready.

Senator SMITH. Any jostling, pushing, or crowding?

Mr. LIGHTOLLER. None whatever.

Senator SMITH. The men all refrained from asserting their strength and crowding back the women and children?

Mr. LIGHTOLLER. They could not have stood quieter if they had been in church.

Senator SMITH. If you had filled that third boat full, how many people would you have had in it?

Mr. LIGHTOLLER. What do you mean by full?

Senator SMITH. To its full capacity.

Mr. LIGHTOLLER. Sixty-five.

Senator SMITH. Beg pardon?

Mr. LIGHTOLLER. Sixty-five, sir.

Senator SMITH. Do you think you had that many in it?

Mr. LIGHTOLLER. Certainly not, sir.

Senator SMITT. How many did you have?

Mr. LIGHTOLLER. Thirty-five, I should say, sir.

Senator SMITH. Thirty-five?

Mr. LIGHTOLLER. About.

Senator SMITH. And two men?

Mr. LIGHTOLLER. Yes.

Senator SMITH. Then the fourth boat. Was there any fourth boat on that side?

Mr. LIGHTOLLER. There were eight boats to a side

Senator SMITH. As to the fourth boat, you followed the same course?

Mr. LIGHTOLLER. The same order; the same conditions.

Senator SMITH. You put two men in each?

Mr. LIGHTOLLER. I think I was getting short of men, if I remember rightly. I started to putting one seaman and a steward in.

Senator SMITH. One seaman and a steward?

Mr. LIGHTOLLER. Yes. That was the boat I had to put a man passenger in. I could only find one seaman. I had started to lower the boat. I had put two seamen in and then I wanted two for lowering. It is absolutely necessary to have a seaman on each fall. No one else can lower a boat. I was calling for seamen, and one of the seamen jumped out of the boat and started to lowering away. The boat was half way down when the women called out and said that there was only one man in the boat. I had only two seamen and could not part with them, and was in rather a fix to know what to do, when a passenger called out and said, "If you like, I will go."

Senator SMITH. Did you know him?

Mr. LIGHTOLLER. I did not.

Senator SMITH. Was he an officer of the ship?

Mr. LIGHTOLLER. No, sir; a first-class passenger.

Senator SMITH. You don't know who he was?

Mr. LIGHTOLLER. I have found out who he was since.

Senator SMITH. Who was he?

Mr. LIGHTOLLER. Maj. Pusey. [Major Arthur Peuchen]

Senator SMITH. Of Toronto?

Mr. LIGHTOLLER. Of Toronto. That is the name, yes.

Senator SMITH. Is he an officer of the British Army?

Mr. LIGHTOLLER. I don't know what he is. He is not a Britisher, anyway.

Senator SMITH. Did he volunteer?

Mr. LIGHTOLLER. No, sir.

Senator SMITH. What did he say?

Mr. LIGHTOLLER. He merely said, "I will go if you like." I said "Are you a seaman," and he said "I am a yachtsman." I said "If you are sailor enough to get out on that fall" - that is a difficult thing to get to, over the ship's side, 8 feet away, and means a long swing on a dark night - "if you are sailor enough to get out there you can go down." And he proved he was, by going down. And he afterwards proved himself a brave man, too.

Senator SMITH. In what respect?

Mr. LIGHTOLLER. From the accounts I heard of him after we were rescued.

Senator SMITH. You mean as to his conduct?

Mr. LIGHTOLLER. As to his conduct.

Senator SMITH. In the lifeboat?

Mr. LIGHTOLLER. In the lifeboat.

Senator SMITH. How old a man was he, about?

Mr. LIGHTOLLER. Forty-five or fifty.

Senator SMITH. Did he have any family with him?

Mr. LIGHTOLLER. I couldn't say, sir.

Senator SMITH. Had you ever seen him before?

Mr. LIGHTOLLER. Never.

Senator SMITH. Have you seen him since?

Mr. LIGHTOLLER. I saw him on the Carpathia. I made it my business to find him.

Senator SMITH. How many did you say you had in this boat?

Mr. LIGHTOLLER. Thirty-five; about the same, as far as I remember.

Senator SMITH. That is the fourth one. How about the fifth?

Mr. LIGHTOLLER. As far as I know, the conditions were the same.

Senator SMITH. Did you have to call somebody from among the passengers?

Mr. LIGHTOLLER. No, sir; I can not remember anything in particular about that boat.

Senator SMITH. About the fifth?

Mr. LIGHTOLLER. No, sir; no particular incident, strikes me. I was getting along then just as fast as ever I could. I was too quick to bother about things.

Senator SMITH. How many women were you caring for? How many did you have aboard the ship?

Mr. LIGHTOLLER. I could not say.

Senator SMITH. Do you know whether they were all cared for?

Mr. LIGHTOLLER. I could not say, sir.

Senator SMITH. All that would go?

Mr. LIGHTOLLER. In the case of the last boat I got out, I had the utmost difficulty in finding women. It was the very last boat of all, after all the other boats were put out and we came forward to put out the collapsible boats. In the meantime the forward emergency boat had been put out by one of the other officers. So we rounded up the tackles and got the collapsible boat to put that over. Then I called for women and could not get hold of any. Somebody said, "There are no women." With this, several men

Senator SMITH. Who said that?

Mr. LIGHTOLLER. I do not know, sir.

Senator SMITH. On what deck was that?

Mr. LIGHTOLLER. On the boat deck.

Senator SMITH. Were all the women supposed to be on the boat deck?

Mr. LIGHTOLLER. Yes, sir; they were supposed to be.

Senator SMITH. Why?

Mr. LIGHTOLLER. Because the boats were there. I might say that previous to putting this Berthon boat out we had lowered a boat from A deck one deck down below. That was through my fault. It was the first boat I had lowered. I was intending to put the passengers in from A deck. On lowering it down I found the windows were closed. So I sent some one down to open the windows and carried on with the other boats, but decided it was not worth while lowering them down, that I could manage just as well from the boat deck. When I came forward from the other boats I loaded that boat from A deck by getting the women out through the windows. My idea in filling the boats there was because there was a wire hawser running along the side of the ship for coaling purposes, and it was handy to tie the boat

in to, to hold it so that nobody could drop between the side of the boat and the ship.

Senator SMITH. Which one was that?

Mr. LIGHTOLLER. That is No. 4; No. 4 boat.

Senator SMITH. That was filled from there?

Mr. LIGHTOLLER. That was filled from there, loaded, and sent away. Then we went to this Berthon boat.

Senator SMITH. In the fifth boat; how many seamen were there?

Mr. LIGHTOLLER. As far as I remember, two seamen.

Senator SMITH. Two?

Mr. LIGHTOLLER. Yes, sir.

Senator SMITH. How many people did you put into it?

Mr. LIGHTOLLER. I might have put a good deal more; I filled her up as much as I could. When I got down to the fifth boat, that was aft.

Senator SMITH. You were still using your best judgement?

Mr. LIGHTOLLER. I was not using very much judgement then; I was filling them up.

Senator SMITH. At that time you felt -

Mr. LIGHTOLLER. I knew it was a question of the utmost speed, to get the boats away.

Senator SMITH. To get them away?

Mr. LIGHTOLLER. Yes, sir.

Senator SMITH. In that situation you were quite sure that they were filled to their capacity?

Mr. LIGHTOLLER. Yes, sir. I don't say to their floating capacity, I don't say 65.

Senator SMITH. But about the same number of persons were in each boat?

Mr. LIGHTOLLER. I should say 35 or 40.

Senator SMITH. Was the sixth one loaded in the same manner?

Mr. LIGHTOLLER. I think the sixth one put down was this one from A deck that I spoke of - no, the fifth one would be from A deck. I think the chief officer, under his direct supervision, lowered a boat from the after end. Of course I can not be absolutely certain. But when I came forward, as I say, I put the one down from A deck which I told you about. Then we went to the Berthon boat, which is the last boat on the port side, the collapsible boat.

Senator SMITH. The fifth boat was lowered in the same manner?

Mr. LIGHTOLLER. Yes, sir. I think it was the fifth from the A deck.

Senator SMITH. With two seamen?

Mr. LIGHTOLLER. Yes.

Senator SMITH. And the balance women.

Mr. LIGHTOLLER. Women and children.

Senator SMITH. Women and children? Up to this time, so far as you recollect, no men had been permitted to get into these boats?

Mr. LIGHTOLLER. None had attempted to do so; no, sir.

Senator SMITH. How about the sixth boat?

Mr. LIGHTOLLER. That is the collapsible, the surfboat?

Senator SMITH. That is the collapsible. Did you take the same course with that?

Mr. LIGHTOLLER. That is a much smaller boat.

Senator SMITH. How many seamen did you put in that?

Mr. LIGHTOLLER. I think there was one seaman and one steward. I could not say.

Senator SMITH. Do you recollect whether there was a light on that boat?

Mr. LIGHTOLLER. No, sir; I was not looking for lights.

Senator SMITH. Do you recollect whether Mrs. Douglas, of Minneapolis, was in that boat?

Mr. LIGHTOLLER. I do not know her at all, sir.

Senator SMITH. Have you had any talk with her about it?

Mr. LIGHTOLLER. Never have spoken to her or seen her, to my knowledge.

Senator SMITH. How many people were put into this sixth boat?

Mr. LIGHTOLLER. Fifteen or perhaps 20. Between 15 and 20.

Senator SMITH. And two seamen?

Mr. LIGHTOLLER. I do not know what seamen -

Senator SMITH. Or one?

Mr. LIGHTOLLER. I think one seaman probably, if I had one seaman there. Perhaps it was two stewards. I do not know, sir.

Senator SMITH. Would the two stewards answer the same purpose?

Mr. LIGHTOLLER. They would have to.

Senator SMITH. Did you select the men to take that boat the same as you had before?

Mr. LIGHTOLLER. You mean whether I ordered them in?

Senator SMITH. Yes.

Mr. LIGHTOLLER. I ordered them in.

Senator SMITH. But you can not recall who they were?

Mr. LIGHTOLLER. I was just thinking. No, not with any degree of certainty.

Senator SMITH. Were any of them officers?

Mr. LIGHTOLLER. No, sir.

Senator SMITH. Did you have any difficulty in filling it?

Mr. LIGHTOLLER. With women; yes, sir; great difficulty.

Senator SMITH. But you filled it to its capacity?

Mr. LIGHTOLLER. I filled it with about 15 or 20 eventually mustered up. It took longer to fill that boat than it did any other boat, notwithstanding that the others had more in them. On two occasions the men thought there were no more women and commenced to get in and then found one or two more and then got out again.

Senator SMITH. How long a time do you think you had been in loading these six boats?

Mr. LIGHTOLLER. I don't know, sir.

Senator SMITH. If it took 15 to 20 minutes to a boat?

Mr. LIGHTOLLER. About an hour and a half.

Senator SMITH. About an hour and a half?

Mr. LIGHTOLLER. That is about right.

Senator SMITH. The vessel must have been going down?

Mr. LIGHTOLLER. I lowered the last boat 10 feet and it was in the water.

Senator SMITH. You lowered it 10 feet and it was in the water?

Mr. LIGHTOLLER. Yes, sir.

Senator SMITH. When you began lowering, the boat was about 60 feet up from the water?

Mr. LIGHTOLLER. Seventy feet.

Senator SMITH. From the water?

Mr. LIGHTOLLER. Yes, sir.

Senator SMITH. I mean the deck.

Mr. LIGHTOLLER. From the deck; exactly, sir.

Senator SMITH. What did you do with the seventh boat?

Mr. LIGHTOLLER. That was the finish.

Senator SMITH. What was that?

Mr. LIGHTOLLER. The seventh boat was the one on top of the quarters.

Senator SMITH. That was the last boat that was lowered by your orders?

Mr. LIGHTOLLER. It was the last. It was not lowered.

Senator SMITH. Did you see Mr. Ismay at that time?

Mr. LIGHTOLLER. Mr. Ismay, as far as I know, from what I have gathered afterwards, was on the starboard side of the deck wholly, helping out there.

Senator SMITH. He did not enter the boat from the port side?

Mr. LIGHTOLLER. No, sir.

Senator SMITH. How many people do you think were in the seventh boat?

Mr. LIGHTOLLER. There were not any in it.

Senator SMITH. I mean the sixth boat?

Mr. LIGHTOLLER. The last collapsible boat?

Senator SMITH. Yes.

Mr. LIGHTOLLER. I say about 15.

Senator SMITH. Wouldn't it hold any more than that?

Mr. LIGHTOLLER. Perhaps 20. They won't hold many. They are canvas. They will not stand many.

Senator SMITH. They won't stand very much?

Mr. LIGHTOLLER. Oh, no, sir.

Senator SMITH. So that they really do not answer the purpose of a lifeboat?

Mr. LIGHTOLLER. They are not as good as a lifeboat; no, sir.

Senator SMITH. Have neither the capacity nor the resistance?

Mr. LIGHTOLLER. No, sir. They are merely stowed in a smaller place. Perhaps you can stow at least three of those where you can stow one lifeboat. You can stow them one on top of the other.

Senator SMITH. So far as your knowledge goes, the lifeboats on the port side consisted of how many lifeboats and how many of those canvas boats?

Mr. LIGHTOLLER. Seven lifeboats, one emergency boat, which is on the same principle as the lifeboat, practically, only it is a smaller and handier boat, and two collapsible boats.

Senator SMITH. The one that was in the tackle was the last boat that was attempted to be lowered on the port side?

Mr. LIGHTOLLER. The collapsible boat?

Senator SMITH. Yes.

Mr. LIGHTOLLER. Yes, sir.

Senator SMITH. How many of the collapsible boats were there altogether on the ship?

Mr. LIGHTOLLER. Four.

Senator SMITH. And 16 of another type?

Mr. LIGHTOLLER. Yes, sir.

Senator SMITH. You must have been painfully aware of the fact that there were not enough boats there to care for that large passenger list, were you not?

Mr. LIGHTOLLER. Yes, sir.

Senator SMITH. Do you know who had charge on the starboard side of the lowering and filling of the boats?

Mr. LIGHTOLLER. No, sir. Merely what I am told.

Senator SMITH. What have you been told about it. May be we can get something from that.

Mr. LIGHTOLLER. As far as I know, and I think it is correct, Mr. Murdoch. Mr. Murdoch was on the starboard side. I was on the port side, and Mr. Murdoch was on the starboard side, and the chief officer was superintending generally, and lowered one or two boats himself.

Senator SMITH. From whom did you get information?

Mr. LIGHTOLLER. Of course, I saw Mr. Murdoch there when finally I had finished on the port side.

Senator SMITH. You went to the starboard side?

Mr. LIGHTOLLER. On top; yes, sir.

Senator SMITH. For the purpose of lowering this -

Mr. LIGHTOLLER. I went over to see if I could assist.

Senator SMITH. And you saw him there?

Mr. LIGHTOLLER. I saw him there.

Senator SMITH. From anything you have been told, did he pursue the same course on the starboard side in reference to the filling of the lifeboats, and the complement of seamen as you did?

Mr. LIGHTOLLER. That I could not say.

Senator SMITH. Was there any rule as to that?

Mr. LIGHTOLLER. No, sir.

Senator SMITH. As to the number of seamen?

Mr. LIGHTOLLER. No, sir; except for boat drill of course, that was not boat drill.

Senator SMITH. What was the number of the ship's crew?

Mr. LIGHTOLLER. Of seamen?

Senator SMITH. Yes.

Mr. LIGHTOLLER. 71 seamen.

Senator SMITH. What constituted the crew besides seamen?

Mr. LIGHTOLLER. Firemen and stewards.

Senator SMITH. And their force?

Mr. LIGHTOLLER. Oh, yes. They mustered up something like 800, perhaps a little under, perhaps a little over. Somewhere around 800. About 800, roughly speaking, firemen and stewards. A little less than 800. The crew altogether is about 850 or 860; that is, including seamen, firemen, and stewards.

Senator SMITH. And you had your full complement on this voyage?

Mr. LIGHTOLLER. As far as I know.

Senator SMITH. How do you account for your inability to get hold of more than nine seamen to man those lifeboats on the port side?

Mr. LIGHTOLLER. Earlier, and before I realized that there was any danger, I told off the boatswain to take some men - I didn't say how many, leaving the man to use his own judgment, to go down below and open the gangway doors in order that some boats could come alongside and be filled to their utmost capacity. He complied with the order, and, so far as I know, went down below, and I did not see him afterwards. That took away a number of men, and we detailed two men for each boat and two men for lowering down.

Senator SMITH. But you did not have two men for each boat, officer. You only had -

Mr. LIGHTOLLER. So far as they will go.

Senator SMITH. You only had nine seamen to seven boats?

Mr. LIGHTOLLER. Well, I have only been telling you approximately. As far as ever I could I put two seamen in a boat. If I didn't have a seaman there I had to put a steward there.

Senator SMITH. I understand that.

167

Mr. LIGHTOLLER. Sometimes there would be three seamen in a boat. As soon as the boats were lowered to the level of the rail, I would detail one man to jump in and ship the rudder, one man to cast adrift the oars, and one man would see that the plugs were in, and it would take three men.

Senator SMITH. You said you chose these men and when the lifeboat is swung out from the ship and lowered it is supposed that she has her full complement of officers and seamen, is it not?

Mr. LIGHTOLLER. She is swung out and lowered to the level of the rail, sir.

Senator SMITH. Level with the rail but not against the rail?

Mr. LIGHTOLLER. No.

Senator SMITH. When you are lowering the lifeboat you are supposed to have filled it to its safe capacity?

Mr. LIGHTOLLER. Lowering it afterwards from the rail down. You see we have to swing it out first of all and lower it until it is level with the rail, so that the people can have one foot on deck and the other foot to step into the boat. They must be level.

Senator SMITH. When you called Maj. Pusey, you had no seamen?

Mr. LIGHTOLLER. Not that I could see, and I couldn't waste time looking for them.

Senator SMITH. When you put the two officers, if I understand you correctly-

Mr. LIGHTOLLER. No officers.

Senator SMITH. Stewards?

Mr. LIGHTOLLER. Stewards.

Senator SMITH. When you put the two stewards into the lifeboat, you had no seamen?

Mr. LIGHTOLLER. If I put two stewards in. As I say, I might have put two stewards in if there were no seamen.

Senator SMITH. How many of the ship's crew survived?

Mr. LIGHTOLLER. Seamen?

Senator SMITH. Seamen and other attaches or employees?

Mr. LIGHTOLLER. Forty-three seamen, 96 stewards and stewardesses, and 71 firemen.

Senator SMITH. Seventy-one firemen?

Mr. LIGHTOLLER. Yes.

Senator SMITH. And how many seamen?

Mr. LIGHTOLLER. Forty-three.

Senator SMITH. So that you lost 28 seamen?

Mr. LIGHTOLLER. Yes.

Senator SMITH. And how many of the crew have been saved altogether? How many survived, altogether?

Mr. LIGHTOLLER. Two hundred and ten.

Senator SMITH. If the same course was followed on the starboard side with the lifeboats that you took on the port side, how were these men saved?

Mr. LIGHTOLLER. I don't know, sir. I know that a great number were taken out of the water. I made it my special business to inquire, and as far as I can gather, for every six people picked out of the water five of them would be firemen or stewards. On our boat, as I have said before, there was Col. Gracie and young Thayer. I think those were the only two passengers.

Senator SMITH. There were no women on the boat?

Mr. LIGHTOLLER. No. I am speaking of the overturned boat.

Senator SMITH. I refer to that. There were no women on your boat?

Mr. LIGHTOLLER. No, sir; these were all taken out of the water and they were firemen and others of the crew.

Senator SMITH. How many were there on that boat?

Mr. LIGHTOLLER. Roughly, about 30. I take that from my own estimate and from the estimate of some one who was looking down from the bridge of the Carpathia.

Senator SMITH. Assuming there were 24 of those among the crew?

Mr. LIGHTOLLER. Yes.

Senator SMITH. That would still leave 190 to get over on these other lifeboats that were filled with women and children?

Mr. LIGHTOLLER. Some of the boats went back and picked up people out of the wreckage after the ship had gone down, mostly firemen and stewards.

Senator SMITH. What boats?

Mr. LIGHTOLLER. Some of the lifeboats.

Senator SMITH. Some of the lifeboats went back?

Mr. LIGHTOLLER. That is what I understand; of course, I don't know.

Senator SMITH. How far would they have gone?

Mr. LIGHTOLLER. I don't know, sir. I am only giving hearsay now.

Senator SMITH. They could not have gone very far. You will recall that the captain of the Carpathia says that the Carpathia did not linger about the scene of the collision but half an hour?

Mr. LIGHTOLLER. They could not have gone very far.

Senator SMITH. These boats would not have gone very far in going back to the scene of the wreck? You do not know of your own knowledge that any of those lifeboats were taken back to the scene of the wreck by anybody?

Mr. LIGHTOLLER. No, sir.

Senator SMITH. As a matter of fact, after rowing these boats as far as they were obliged to row them, in some instances several hours, would they have had little strength to have rowed back, would they not, assuming that the men did the work?

Mr. LIGHTOLLER. I know that they went back, because the men have told me that they were picked up out of the wreckage by the lifeboats that went back.

Senator SMITH. Of your own knowledge you don't know anything about these lifeboats returning?

Mr. LIGHTOLLER. No, sir.

Senator SMITH. From what you have said, you discriminated entirely in the interest of the passengers - first the women and children - in filling those lifeboats?

Mr. LIGHTOLLER. Yes, sir.

Senator SMITH. Why did you do that? Because of the captain's orders, or because of the rule of the sea?

Mr. LIGHTOLLER. The rule of human nature.

Senator SMITH. The rule of human nature? And there was no studied purpose, as far as you know, to save the crew?

Mr. LIGHTOLLER. Absolutely not.

Senator SMITH. The fact that you only put nine seamen into the boats that you lowered, which were half the entire complement-

Mr. LIGHTOLLER. No, sir.

Senator SMITH. One-third?

Mr. LIGHTOLLER. About a third; perhaps a little more than a third; not half.

Senator SMITH. A little more than half when you consider that you did not fill the boat that was on the officers' quarters that was thrown without passengers into the sea?

Mr. LIGHTOLLER. Yes, sir.

Senator SMITH. And one other boat was so entangled in the gearing that it was useless?

Mr. LIGHTOLLER. Yes, sir.

Senator SMITH. That left 18?

Mr. LIGHTOLLER. Yes.

Senator SMITH. Did I understand you to say that 1 of the 18 was injured?

Mr. LIGHTOLLER. (interrupting). Yes, you are right; I beg your pardon.

Senator SMITH. So that this really was a little more than half?

Mr. LIGHTOLLER. I had not thought that I put out half because I am under the impression that the chief officer put out a couple of the after ones on my deck, as well as supervising. He evidently found that he had the time, and put out a couple of these boats, and he also lowered the emergency boat; so I, think it is 3 he put out, out of 10 on that side. That left me 7. I think that is about what I put out; 7.

Senator SMITH. Did I ask you how many women and children there were aboard ship?

Mr. LIGHTOLLER. You did, sir.

Senator SMITH. Did you reply?

Mr. LIGHTOLLER. I do not know.

Senator SMITH. Is there any record available here of the exact number of passengers - men, women, and children? Mr. Franklin, have you that?

Mr. FRANKLIN. That will be furnished.

Senator SMITH. But you are quite clear that there were no women that you could put into the last boat to fill it?

Mr. LIGHTOLLER. Not within my sight and hearing.

Senator SMITH. You were on the boat deck?

Mr. LIGHTOLLER. I was standing in the boat. Oh, I do know the steward that went in the boat now.

Senator SMITH. Tell me who he was.

Mr. LIGHTOLLER. I do not know that I could give his name. If he is here now, I could recognize him if I saw him.

Senator SMITH. That was in the fourth boat?

Mr. LIGHTOLLER. No; the last boat to be lowered in the tackles; the very last boat to be lowered in the tackles.

Senator SMITH. The sixth boat?

Mr. LIGHTOLLER. Yes, sir. I could not tell you his name now, but I know there was a steward there.

Senator SMITH. Did he survive?

Mr. LIGHTOLLER. Yes.

Senator SMITH. Did you notice any Americans?

Mr. LIGHTOLLER. A plenty.

Senator SMITH. Standing near you?

Mr. LIGHTOLLER. Any amount.

Senator SMITH. When you were lowering the women?

Mr. LIGHTOLLER. Any amount. They gave me every assistance they could, regardless of nationality.

Senator SMITH. Did you hear any of their names?

Mr. LIGHTOLLER. What do you mean? At that time, sir?

Senator SMITH. Yes.

Mr. LIGHTOLLER. No, sir.

Senator SMITH. Did any of them attempt to give you their names?

Mr. LIGHTOLLER. No, sir.

Senator SMITH. Do you recall, from anything that you heard on shipboard, the names of any that you may have seen?

Mr. LIGHTOLLER. No; we are not brought in contact with the passengers at all beyond going our rounds.

Senator SMITH. Is it the custom, or was it the custom of your line to print a list of the prominent passengers?

Mr. LIGHTOLLER. No, sir.

Senator SMITH. Or the passengers in a little leaflet?

Mr. LIGHTOLLER. Yes, sir.

Senator SMITH. The first or second day out?

Mr. LIGHTOLLER. Yes, sir.

Senator SMITH. Was this done?

Mr. LIGHTOLLER. Yes; it is done as far as possible before we leave home.

Senator SMITH. But it is not put out until after the ship has been to sea for a day or two, it is?

Mr. LIGHTOLLER. I think it is possibly put out the day of sailing, sir, but really; I could not answer that question.

Senator SMITH. I wonder if we can obtain it.

Mr. FRANKLIN. There is always one out the day of sailing, and there is a corrected one out later. We can give you the one out the day of sailing.

Senator SMITH. That is the one I would like.

Mr. FRANKLIN. Whether we can get you the corrected one or not is an open problem.

Senator SMITH. I will ask you with what type of davit was the Titanic equipped?

174

Mr. LIGHTOLLER. What is known as the Welin patent.

Senator SMITH. Where were those passengers or people congregated when you last saw the Titanic? Were they huddled together into any special part of the ship?

Mr. LIGHTOLLER. No, sir.

Senator SMITH. In sinking, did the ship tilt?

Mr. LIGHTOLLER. Yes, sir.

Senator SMITH. To the fore?

Mr. LIGHTOLLER. Yes, sir.

Senator SMITH. How much?

Mr. LIGHTOLLER. Well, roughly, the crow's nest was level with the water when the bridge went under water.

Senator SMITH. The crow's nest, at the fore point?

Mr. LIGHTOLLER. That is on the foremast. The lookout cage.

Senator SMITH. The crow's nest at the highest point?

Mr. LIGHTOLLER. Yes, sir.

Senator SMITH. Was in the water?

Mr. LIGHTOLLER. Was just about level with the water.

Senator SMITH. When the bridge was submerged?

Mr. LIGHTOLLER. Yes, sir.

Senator SMITH. And about what was the angle?

Mr. LIGHTOLLER. I am afraid I could hardly tell you the angle, sir.

Mr. KIRLIN. Get the plan and find the height of the crow's nest above the deck, and that would give it.

Mr. LIGHTOLLER. The plan showing the height of the crow's nest and the bridge would give it to you, roughly.

Senator SMITH. I ask you again. There must have been a great number of passengers and crew still on the boat, the part of the boat that was not submerged, probably on the high point, so far as possible. Were they huddled together?

Mr. LIGHTOLLER. I could not say, sir. They did not seem to be. I could not say, sir; I did not notice; there were a great many of them; there was a great many of them, I know, but as to what condition they were in, huddled or not, I do not know.

Senator SMITH. Did they make any demonstration?

Mr. LIGHTOLLER. None.

Senator SMITH. Was there any lamentation?

Mr. LIGHTOLLER. No, sir; not a sign of it.

Senator SMITH. There must have been about 2,000 people there on that part - the unsubmerged part of the boat?

Mr. LIGHTOLLER. All the engineers and other men and many of the firemen were down below and never came on deck at all.

Senator SMITH. They never came on deck?

Mr. LIGHTOLLER. No, sir; they were never seen. That would reduce it by a great number.

Senator SMITH. After this impact, did you hear any explosion of any kind?

Mr. LIGHTOLLER. None whatever, sir.

Senator SMITH. What would be the effect of water at about zero -

Mr. LIGHTOLLER (interposing): At about freezing?

Senator SMITH. What would be the effect of water at about freezing on the boilers?

Mr. LIGHTOLLER. It is an open question. I have heard it said that they will explode, and others say they will not.

Senator SMITH. Have you ever known of a case?

Mr. LIGHTOLLER. Of a case in point?

Senator SMITH. Where they have exploded?

Mr. LIGHTOLLER. I was sucked down, and I was blown out with something pretty powerful when the ship went down.

Senator SMITH. After the ship went down?

Mr. LIGHTOLLER. Yes.

Senator SMITH. Just describe that a little more fully. You were sucked down?

Mr. LIGHTOLLER. I was sucked against the blower first of all. As I say, I was on top of the officers' quarters, and there was nothing more to be done. The ship then took a dive, and I turned face forward and also took a dive.

Senator SMITH. From which side?

Mr. LIGHTOLLER. From on top, practically midships; a little to the starboard side, where I had got to; and I was driven back against a blower - which is a large thing that shape [indicating] which faces forward to the wind and which then goes down to the stokehole. But there is a grating there, and it was against this grating that I was sucked by the water and held there.

Senator SMITH. Was your head above water?

Mr. LIGHTOLLER. No, sir.

Senator SMITH. You were under water?

Mr. LIGHTOLLER. Yes, sir. And then this explosion, or whatever it was, took place. Certainly, I think it was the boilers exploded. There was a terrific blast of air and water, and I was blown out clear.

Senator SMITH. Was there any debris that was blown above the surface?

Mr. LIGHTOLLER. That I could not say.

Senator SMITH. At least you took your head out of the water?

Mr. LIGHTOLLER. I came up above the water; yes.

Senator SMITH. And how far from the sinking ship did it throw you?

Mr. LIGHTOLLER. Barely threw me away at all; barely threw me away at all, because I went down again against these fiddley gratings immediately abreast of the funnel over the stokehole

Senator SMITH. Was anybody else sucked down at the time?

Mr. LIGHTOLLER. Col. Gracie, I believe, was sucked down in identically the same manner. He was sucked down on the fiddley gratings.

Senator SMITH. There must have been considerable suction?

Mr. LIGHTOLLER. That was the water rushing down below as she was going down.

Senator SMITH. Going down into the ship?

Mr. LIGHTOLLER. Exactly.

Senator SMITH. How did you get released from that?

Mr. LIGHTOLLER. Oh, I don't know, sir. I think it was the boilers again, but I do not distinctly remember. I do not know.

Senator SMITH. Where did you next find yourself?

Mr. LIGHTOLLER. Alongside of that raft.

Senator SMITH. Where?

Mr. LIGHTOLLER. Alongside of that upturned boat that had been launched on the other side.

Senator SMITH. Where had you gone at that time? Had you gone around the ship?

Mr. LIGHTOLLER. No, sir; the boat had come around.

Senator SMITH. Was there anyone on it?

Mr. LIGHTOLLER. I don't think so. I think they were around it.

Senator SMITH. Your position had not changed, but the boat's position had?

Mr. LIGHTOLLER. Yes, sir.

Senator SMITH. Were there any water-tight compartments in that ship?

Mr. LIGHTOLLER. Yes, sir.

Senator SMITH. How many?

Mr. LIGHTOLLER. I could not tell you offhand, sir: 40 or 50.

Senator SMITH. Nearly 50?

Mr. LIGHTOLLER. I say 40 or 50; I can not tell you offhand

Senator SMITH. How were they constructed?

Mr. LIGHTOLLER. They were divisional bulkheads; water-tight doors, operated by electricity or mechanically.

Senator SMITH. Were those water-tight compartments known to the passengers or crew?

Mr. LIGHTOLLER. They must have been.

Senator SMITH. How would they know it?

Mr. LIGHTOLLER. By the plans distributed about the ship.

Senator SMITH. Were they advised at any time that there were water-tight compartments - about how many?

Mr. LIGHTOLLER. Forty or fifty.

Senator SMITH. Were they advised that there were 40 or 50 water-tight compartments?

Mr. LIGHTOLLER. I could not say, sir.

Senator SMITH. You heard nothing of that kind and gave no such warning yourself?

Mr. LIGHTOLLER. No, sir.

Senator SMITH. Are you able to say whether any of the crew or passengers took to these upper water-tight compartments as a final, last resort; I mean as a place to die?

Mr. LIGHTOLLER. I am quite unable to say, sir.

Senator SMITH. Is that at all likely?

Mr. LIGHTOLLER. No, sir; very unlikely.

Senator SMITH. As for yourself, you preferred to take your chance in the open sea?

Mr. LIGHTOLLER. Undoubtedly.

Senator SMITH. Where were those compartments with reference to the boat deck?

Mr. LIGHTOLLER. Below the boat deck, sir.

Senator SMITH. How far below?

Mr. LIGHTOLLER. They extend from the bottom of the ship about four decks up.

Senator SMITH. Would they extend up as high as 50 feet?

Mr. LIGHTOLLER. About that.

Senator SMITH. Above the water?

Mr. LIGHTOLLER. Oh, they are above the water line; they extend above the water line.

Senator SMITH. Are they all above the water line?

Mr. LIGHTOLLER. No, sir; from the bottom of the ship up to above the water line.

Senator SMITH. Have you been in any of the water-tight compartments of the Titanic?

Mr. LIGHTOLLER. I have been in all of them.

Senator SMITH. What are these doors made of?

Mr. LIGHTOLLER.   As far as I understand, of metal for that purpose.

Senator SMITH.   And how are they fastened? Are they locked by bar, or bolt, or key?

Mr. LIGHTOLLER.   The lower section of the water-tight doors fore and aft the ship are operated by electricity and they automatically lock themselves, and can not be touched whilst the current is on.

Senator SMITH. How can they be opened?

Mr. LIGHTOLLER.   By switching the current off and opening them by hand down below.

Senator SMITH.   If there were no current how could they be opened?

Mr. LIGHTOLLER.   By hand.

Senator SMITH.   In what manner?

Mr. LIGHTOLLER.   By ratchet and screw, lever and cogwheel.

Senator SMITH.   A person would have to be rather familiar with that construction in order to open them?

Mr. LIGHTOLLER.   No, sir; the handle is right alongside every door, and the manner for opening them is obvious.

Senator SMITH.   But when the doors are closed and the current is on?

Mr. LIGHTOLLER. I am only speaking of those at the bottom of the ship.

Senator SMITH.   Let us go up a little higher, and tell me about the doors, and the construction there.

Mr. LIGHTOLLER. They are operated by hand, closed by lever. They can be closed from the deck above, or from the deck you are on. There is a specially constructed key that fits into the deck above. When you turn it around, the door closes. One man can close or open it.

Senator SMITH. You must first have a key?

Mr. LIGHTOLLER. Yes; keys are kept alongside of the doors. When the door is closed it so engages a system or series of wedges that it is water tight.

Senator SMITH. What are those water-tight compartments for?

Mr. LIGHTOLLER. To shut out the water, retaining the water in one compartment, to prevent its going fore and aft the ship.

Senator SMITH. How much of the ship had gone down when you left it?

Mr. LIGHTOLLER. I went under water on top of the officers' quarters, immediately at the fore part of the forward funnel; so she was under water at the fore part of the forward funnel.

Senator NEWLANDS. You say that after you came up you attached yourself to this raft the funnel fell upon those who were upon one side of the raft?

Mr. LIGHTOLLER. I say the funnel fell down, and if anybody was on that side of the raft it fell on them.

Senator NEWLANDS. Then by that time the entire ship was not submerged?

Mr. LIGHTOLLER. Oh,, dear, no; not by considerable.

Senator NEWLANDS. What portion of the ship was out of water at that time?

Mr. LIGHTOLLER. The stern of the ship was completely out of the water.

Senator SMITH. It was out of water, at an angle?

Senator NEWLANDS. Yes, I see.

Senator SMITH. What other officers besides yourself survived?

Mr. LIGHTOLLER. The third, fourth, and fifth, sir.

Senator SMITH. Will you kindly give their names?

Mr. LIGHTOLLER. Mr. Pitman, third officer; Mr. Boxhall, fourth officer; and Mr. Lowe, fifth officer.

Senator SMITH. You had better give their initials.

Mr. LIGHTOLLER. Mr. H. J. Pitman, third officer; Mr. J. G. Boxhall, fourth officer; and Mr. G. Lowe, fifth officer.

TESTIMONY OF HAROLD THOMAS COTTAM.

Marconi Operator, SS Carpathia

The witness was sworn by the chairman.

Senator SMITH. Mr. Cottam, what is your full name?

Mr. COTTAM. Harold Thomas Cottam.

Senator SMITH. Where do you reside?

Mr. COTTAM. Liverpool, England.

Senator SMITH. How old are you?

Mr. COTTAM. Twenty-one.

Senator SMITH. What is your business?

Mr. COTTAM. Marconi telegraphist.

Senator SMITH. How long have you been engaged in that business?

Mr. COTTAM. Three years.

Senator SMITH. Where have you been employed?

Mr. COTTAM. The Marconi Co. all the time.

Senator SMITH. How extensively; that is, how many different employments?

Mr. COTTAM. I went to sea first. Then I was taken off there and worked for the British post office for a time.

Senator SMITH. In what capacity?

Mr. COTTAM. As telegraphist, on one of their land stations.

Senator SMITH. Under the British post-office authorities?

Mr. COTTAM. Yes, sir.

Senator SMITH. Where?

Mr. COTTAM. Liverpool.

Senator SMITH. How long were you thus employed?

Mr. COTTAM. About 14 to 16 months.

Senator SMITH. Then what did you do?

Mr. COTTAM. I was taken off there and went away to sea again, on the Australian run.

Senator SMITH. On. what boat?

Mr. COTTAM. The Medic, White Star.

Senator SMITH. How long were you on the Medic?

Mr. COTTAM. Two voyages.

Senator SMITH. Were you wireless telegrapher at that time?

Mr. COTTAM. Yes, sir.

Senator SMITH. Two voyages?

Mr. COTTAM. Yes, sir.

Senator SMITH. Out and right back?

Mr. COTTAM. Yes; return voyages.

Senator SMITH. From Liverpool.

Mr. COTTAM. To Australia and back to Liverpool again.

Senator SMITH. What kind of apparatus was there on the Medic?

Mr. COTTAM. A Marconi, sir.

Senator SMITH. What type of instrument or equipment?

Mr. COTTAM. A one and a half watt set, sir.

Senator SMITH. What was the maximum wave length?

Mr. COTTAM. A standard wave length, sir; 2,000 feet.

Senator SMITH. You were in charge of the wireless on that boat?

Mr. COTTAM. Yes.

Senator SMITH. Chief in charge?

Mr. COTTAM. Only one man, sir.

Senator SMITH. What was your next employment?

Mr. COTTAM. On the Carpathia, sir.

Senator SMITH. How long were you on the Carpathia?

Mr. COTTAM. I joined her in Liverpool, last February, sir.

Senator SMITH. You have been with the Carpathia ever since?

Mr. COTTAM. Yes, sir.

Senator SMITH. Did you ship with her from New York?

Mr. COTTAM. From Liverpool, sir.

Senator SMITH. From New York the other day?

Mr. COTTAM. Yes, sir.

Senator SMITH. What day?

Mr. COTTAM. I do not remember the day. About the 10th or 11th, I think, sir.

Senator SMITH. On her last outward voyage?

Mr. COTTAM. Yes, sir.

Senator SMITH. Where was she headed for?

Mr. COTTAM. Gibraltar, sir.

Senator SMITH. Did she have a wireless equipment?

Mr. COTTAM. Yes, sir.

Senator SMITH. What kind?

Mr. COTTAM. Marconi, sir.

Senator SMITH. Up-to-date equipment?

Mr. COTTAM. No, sir; it was an older type.

Senator SMITH. What was the maximum distance with which that equipment could be operated successfully?

Mr. COTTAM. Two hundred and fifty miles.

Senator SMITH. Did you obtain satisfactory results from 250-mile experiments?

Mr. COTTAM. Yes, sir.

Senator SMITH. On the Carpathia?

Mr. COTTAM. Yes, sir.

Senator SMITH. You were on the boat last Sunday?

Mr. COTTAM. Yes, sir.

Senator SMITH. What were your hours of employment?

Mr. COTTAM. There are no stated hours. There is only one man on the boat.

Senator SMITH. I understand; but what periods during the day and night are you expected to be at your instrument?

Mr. COTTAM. It all depends on where you are. If you were in the vicinity of New York or thereabouts you would be expected to be on duty all the time.

Senator SMITH. Night and day?

Mr. COTTAM. Yes, sir.

Senator SMITH. Is that practicable?

Mr. COTTAM. Yes, sir.

Senator SMITH. In making the voyage from New York to Gibraltar, after you have gotten out to sea, there is no rigid rule which requires you to be at your post?

Mr. COTTAM. No, sir.

Senator SMITH. No regulation of the British Government?

Mr. COTTAM. No, sir.

Senator SMITH. No direction by the Marconi Co.?

Mr. COTTAM. No, sir; but you are more or less responsible for communications which are expected.

Senator SMITH. You are responsible for communication?

Mr. COTTAM. Yes, sir; if there is a ship expected, sir. If a ship is expected to pass at 3 o'clock in the morning you should be at duty at that time to establish communication.

Senator SMITH. Has it been your custom to go to the apparatus at regular times?

Mr. COTTAM. No, sir.

Senator SMITH. Are you employed at anything else on the boat?

Mr. COTTAM. No, sir.

Senator SMITH. What wages do you receive?

Mr. COTTAM. Four pounds ten a month.

Senator SMITH. Four pounds ten shillings a month?

Mr. COTTAM. Yes, sir.

Senator SMITH. And board?

Mr. COTTAM. Yes, sir.

Senator SMITH. And room?

Mr. COTTAM. The room is attached to the operating room.

Senator SMITH. Is that the average wage of wireless telegraphers in England?

Mr. COTTAM. I can not say that it is.

Senator SMITH. To whom do you report aboard ship?

Mr. COTTAM. To the captain.

Senator SMITH. Personally?

Mr. COTTAM. Yes.

Senator SMITH. And from whom do you take orders?

Mr. COTTAM. From the captain, sir.

Senator SMITH. Personally.

Mr. COTTAM. Yes.

Senator SMITH. From anyone else?

Mr. COTTAM. No, sir.

Senator SMITH. From the officer on watch? Do you take orders from him?

Mr. COTTAM. No, sir; not without I have the authority of the captain.

Senator SMITH. Not without the direction of the captain?

Mr. COTTAM. No.

Senator SMITH. Would you take orders from anyone except the captain of the ship while you were aboard ship? Suppose Mr. Marconi or some officer of the Marconi Co. gave orders to you by wireless which you should pick up, would you consider it your duty to take them from the officers of the Marconi Co. while you were at sea?

Mr. COTTAM. Not before the captain of the ship, sir.

Senator SMITH. Then I am to understand you have no specified hours when you shall be in attendance at your instrument?

Mr. COTTAM. During the whole of the day, sir; not necessarily at night.

Senator SMITH. During all the day?

Mr. COTTAM. The whole of the day, daytime, but not at nights.

Senator SMITH. Do you have liberty to retire at nights when you please?

Mr. COTTAM. Yes, sir.

Senator SMITH. And what has been your custom in that regard, what time would you retire?

Mr. COTTAM. While at sea I should retire about midnight.

Senator SMITH. Where is this instrument located on the ship?

Mr. COTTAM. In the Carpathia, sir?

Senator SMITH. Yes, where?

Mr. COTTAM. On the after part of the ship.

Senator SMITH. On what deck?

Mr. COTTAM. On an island above the second-class smoking room.

Senator SMITH. What have you there, a room?

Mr. COTTAM. Yes, sir.

Senator SMITH. Or two rooms?

Mr. COTTAM. One room.

Senator SMITH. And you say you were at liberty to retire at night when you please?

Mr. COTTAM. Everything depends on circumstances.

Senator SMITH. What would it depend on?

Mr. COTTAM. If I had work to get off and I could not get it off before the early hours of the morning I should have to stay up to attend it.

Senator SMITH.. That is commercial work?

Mr. COTTAM. Yes, sir.

Senator SMITH. Sending messages for your passengers?

Mr. COTTAM. Or for the captain; yes, sir.

Senator SMITH. At night you are not open for commercial business?

Mr. COTTAM. Never have done it; only with the captain, sir.

Senator SMITH. Or official business?

Mr. COTTAM. Yes, sir.

Senator SMITH. Are you able to get the best results in the daytime or in the night ordinarily?

Mr. COTTAM. In the night.

Senator SMITH. Can you tell why that is - why that is so?

Mr. COTTAM. Owing to a certain state of the atmosphere. I do not know what the state is.

Senator SMITH. And yet at night you undertake to do no business, or are your customers lacking at night?

Mr. COTTAM. Yes, sir.

Senator SMITH. The passengers on the boat do not seek to do business at night?

Mr. COTTAM. No, sir.

Senator SMITH. Have you any rules which require you to use your instrument or put it in position to be used for distress calls every hour of the day or any hour of the day?

Mr. COTTAM. There is nothing in the Marconi system that would detect the signals if the operator is not present.

Senator SMITH. That is, no warning or alarm?

Mr. COTTAM. No, sir.

Senator SMITH. Is that true of the more modern equipment?

Mr. COTTAM. Yes, sir.

Senator SMITH. They have an alarm?

Mr. COTTAM. No, sir.

Senator SMITH. They have none?

Mr. COTTAM. No, sir.

Senator SMITH. What were you doing last Sunday evening about 10 o'clock?

Mr. COTTAM. Receiving the news from Cape Cod, the long-distance station.

Senator SMITH. Receiving news from Cape Cod?

Mr. COTTAM. Yes, sir.

Senator SMITH. What kind of news?

Mr. COTTAM. General news.

Senator SMITH. General news for the accommodation for passengers on ship?

Mr. COTTAM. Yes, sir.

Senator SMITH. Have you specified hours for that purpose?

Mr. COTTAM. We are not obliged to take the news, sir.

Senator SMITH. You are not obliged to take it?

Mr. COTTAM. That is right.

Senator SMITH. But on this occasion you did take it?

Mr. COTTAM. Yes, sir.

Senator SMITH. How long did you take it?

Mr. COTTAM. I did not start to take it.

Senator SMITH. How far were you from Cape Cod?

Mr. COTTAM. I could not tell you the exact distance.

Senator SMITH. About how far? What was the required wave length? Can you tell, or did you do any sending?

Mr. COTTAM. No transmitting.

Senator SMITH. No transmitting; just receiving?

Mr. COTTAM. Yes, sir.

Senator SMITH. After you finished the Cape Cod business, what did you do then?

Mr. COTTAM. At the latter end of the news from Cape Cod, he was sending a lot of messages for the Titanic.

Senator SMITH. What time was that?

Mr. COTTAM. About 11 o'clock.

Senator SMITH. What had you been doing just preceding the message from the Titanic?

Mr. COTTAM. Reporting the day's communications to the bridge.

Senator SMITH. Had you closed your station for the night?

Mr. COTTAM. No.

Senator SMITH. What do you do when you close your station; anything?

Mr. COTTAM. No; there is nothing particular done.

Senator SMITH. Nothing?

Mr. COTTAM. No.

Senator SMITH. You do not have to detach any battery wires?

Mr. COTTAM. Switch the charging battery out, the storage battery. We switch that out for the night.

Senator SMITH. Switch the storage battery out?

Mr. COTTAM. Yes.

Senator SMITH. Does that "kill" the instrument?

Mr. COTTAM. No.

Senator SMITH. Can you receive messages with that out?

Mr. COTTAM. Yes.

Senator SMITH. But you can not send them?

Mr. COTTAM. Yes.

Senator SMITH. You can both receive and send them?

Mr. COTTAM. Yes.

Senator SMITH. Well then what in reality have you done when you shift this battery connection?

Mr. COTTAM. I have taken them off charge, sir.

Senator SMITH. Does that lessen the likelihood of your getting any signal of any kind?

Mr. COTTAM. No, sir; not in the least.

Senator SMITH. I believe you told us how far this equipment on the Carpathia would send a message with accuracy, did you not?

Mr. COTTAM. Yes, sir.

Senator SMITH. About 250 miles, I think you said?

Mr. COTTAM. Yes.

Senator SMITH. Was there any thunder or lightning or cloud that night?

Mr. COTTAM. No.

Senator SMITH. Sunday night?

Mr. COTTAM. No, sir.

Senator SMITH. It was clear?

Mr. COTTAM. Yes, sir.

Senator SMITH. How did you happen to catch this communication from the Titanic?

Mr. COTTAM. I was looking out for the Parisian, to confirm a previous communication with the Parisian.

Senator SMITH. You had been in communication with the Parisian that day?

Mr. COTTAM. Yes, sir.

Senator SMITH. At what time?

Mr. COTTAM. I can not say. At some time in the afternoon, sir.

Senator SMITH. Not a distress signal?

Mr. COTTAM. Oh, no, sir.

Senator SMITH. Some commercial or business communication?

Mr. COTTAM. Yes, sir.

Senator SMITH. How far was the Parisian from you?

Mr. COTTAM. I do not know, sir.

Senator SMITH. You have no means of knowing?

Mr. COTTAM. No, sir.

Senator SMITH. Her position was not stated?

Mr. COTTAM. No, sir.

Senator SMITH. You ad been in communication with the Parisian that afternoon?

Mr. COTTAM. Yes, sir.

Senator SMITH. And this Sunday evening you were looking out for further communication from that boat?

Mr. COTTAM. No, sir.

Senator SMITH. Well, how did you happen to be at your instrument?

Mr. COTTAM. I say, I was confirming, or attempting to confirm a previous communication with the Parisian - I was not sure of her communication.

Senator SMITH. Did you hear the captain of the Carpathia to-day?

Mr. COTTAM. No, sir.

Senator SMITH. He said you were about to retire.

Mr. COTTAM. Yes, sir.

Senator SMITH. And caught this message rather providentially?

Mr. COTTAM. Yes, sir.

Senator SMITH. How far had you gotten along in your arrangements to retire?

Mr. COTTAM. Well, I was about to retire.

Senator SMITH. Had you disrobed - taken all your clothes?

Mr. COTTAM. No, sir.

Senator SMITH. Had you taken off your shoes?

Mr. COTTAM. No, sir.

Senator: SMITH: Had you taken off any of your clothing?

Mr. COTTAM. I had my coat off.

Senator SMITH. When you took your coat off, did you have any instruments attached to your head?

196

Mr. COTTAM. Yes, sir.

Senator SMITH. What?

Mr. COTTAM. Telephones.

Senator SMITH. How did you happen to leave that on?

Mr. COTTAM. I was waiting for the Parisian.

Senator SMITH. How long would you have waited; just long enough to undress?

Mr. COTTAM. I would have waited a couple of minutes. I had just called the Parisian and was waiting for a reply, if there was one.

Senator SMITH. And you had just called her?

Mr. COTTAM. Yes.

Senator SMITH. And you did not know whether she had gotten it or not?

Mr. COTTAM. No, sir.

Senator SMITH. And you were waiting for an acknowledgement?

Mr. COTTAM. Yes, sir.

Senator SMITH. So you kept this telephone on your ears, on your head?

Mr. COTTAM. Yes, sir.

Senator SMITH. On your head?

Mr. COTTAM. Yes.

Senator SMITH. With the hope that before you got into bed you might have your message confirmed?

Mr. COTTAM. Yes, sir.

Senator SMITH. Was that what you had in mind?

Mr. COTTAM. Yes, sir.

Senator SMITH. What did you hear at that time?

Mr. COTTAM. I heard nothing, sir.

Senator SMITH. How soon? You heard something pretty quick, did you not?

Mr. COTTAM. No, sir; I went back onto Cape Cod again.

Senator SMITH. And still left this apparatus on?

Mr. COTTAM. Yes, sir.

Senator SMITH. Did you send a message to Cape Cod?

Mr. COTTAM. No, sir.

Senator SMITH. Did Cape Cod send a message to you?

Mr. COTTAM. No, sir.

Senator SMITH. Then, as a matter of fact, you did not get back to Cape Cod?

Mr. COTTAM. Yes, sir.

Senator SMITH. How?

Mr. COTTAM. They were sending it for the trans-Atlantic two-man ships. They were sending the news to the senior ships.

Senator SMITH. Where?

Mr. COTTAM. These ships that contribute to the Marconi press.

Senator SMITH. An intermediate communication, intermediate station?

Mr. COTTAM. No, sir; Cape Cod, which is the Atlantic station.

Senator SMITH. You got into communication?

Mr. COTTAM. Yes, sir.

Senator SMITH. With one of the Marconi stations?

Mr. COTTAM. I did not establish it. I was receiving the press communications from Cape Cod.

Senator SMITH. While you were undressing there?

Mr. COTTAM. I was not undressing.

Senator SMITH. After you had taken off your coat?

Mr. COTTAM: Yes, sir.

Senator SMITH. And then did you sit down to your instrument?

Mr. COTTAM. Yes, sir.

Senator SMITH. And received this message?

Mr. COTTAM. I received about four.

Senator SMITH. In how many minutes?

Mr. COTTAM. About seven or eight minutes.

Senator SMITH. You received four in seven or eight minutes?

Mr. COTTAM. Yes, sir.

Senator SMITH. Did that include anything from the Parisian?

Mr. COTTAM. No, sir.

Senator SMITH. Simply this Cape Cod relay service?

Mr. COTTAM. Yes, sir; sending messages for the Titanic. I was taking the messages down with the hope of re-transmitting them the following morning.

Senator SMITH. Let us understand that a little. When did you first know anything about the Titanic?

Mr. COTTAM. I had had communication with her late in the afternoon, half past 5 or 6.

Senator SMITH. A stray communication, or one addressed to the Carpathia?

Mr. COTTAM. One addressed to the Carpathia.

Senator SMITH. What did it say?

Mr. COTTAM. It was a message for one of our passengers aboard.

Senator SMITH. For whom?

Mr. COTTAM. Mrs. Marshal.

Senator SMITH.   A commercial message, an official message?

Mr. COTTAM. A commercial message.

Senator SMITH.   So that was the only message you received from the Titanic in the afternoon. Was the message answered?

Mr. COTTAM. Yes, sir.

Senator SMITH. Do you know anything about how far you were from her at that time?

Mr. COTTAM. No, sir.

Senator SMITH. Have you no means of knowing?

Mr. COTTAM. No, sir.

Senator SMITH.   After you got through with this regular business, then what did you do?

Mr. COTTAM. I called the Titanic.

Senator SMITH. You called the Titanic yourself?

Mr. COTTAM. Yes, sir.

Senator SMITH. Who told you to do it?

Mr. COTTAM.   I did it of my own free will.

Senator SMITH. You did it of your own accord?

Mr. COTTAM. Yes, sir.

Senator SMITH. What did you say?

Mr. COTTAM. I asked him if he was aware that Cape Cod was sending a batch of messages for him.

Senator SMITH. And did they reply?

Mr. COTTAM. Yes, sir.

Senator SMITH. What did they say?

Mr. COTTAM.   "Come at once."

Senator SMITH.   Did you gather from that that they had received your communication?

Mr. COTTAM. Yes, sir.

Senator SMITH; And this was the reply?

Mr. COTTAM. He said, "Come at once. It is a distress message; C. Q. D."

Senator SMITH. Only the three words were used?

Mr. COTTAM. No, sir, all the lot. The whole message was for me.

Senator SMITH. When you received that message, what did you do?

Mr. COTTAM: I confirmed it by asking him if I was to report it to the captain.

Senator SMITH. Before you reported to the captain you asked him if you were to report it to the captain?

Mr. COTTAM. Yes, sir.

Senator SMITH. Did you get an answer?

Mr. COTTAM. Yes, sir.

Senator SMITH. What did it say?

Mr. COTTAM. It said, "Yes."

Senator SMITH. How did you happen to confirm it?

Mr. COTTAM. By asking him if -

Senator SMITH (interrupting): I know, but what prompted you to confirm it before you delivered it to the captain?

Mr. COTTAM. Because it is always wise to confirm a message of that description.

Senator SMITH. Do you always do it?

Mr. COTTAM. Yes, sir.

Senator SMITH. Are you instructed to do it?

Mr. COTTAM. No, sir.

Senator SMITH. Or is that a matter of discretion?

Mr. COTTAM. It is a matter of discretion.

Senator SMITH. Had you been misled by messages that were without foundation that prompted you to confirm that message?

Mr. COTTAM. No, sir.

Senator SMITH. What would you have done if you had not received any confirmation?

Mr. COTTAM. I should have reported the communication.

Senator SMITH. You would have reported it to the captain?

Mr. COTTAM. Yes, sir.

Senator SMITH. How much time elapsed between the time when you received that distress call and the time you communicated it to the captain?

Mr. COTTAM. A matter of a couple of minutes.

Senator SMITH. Only a couple of minutes?

Mr. COTTAM. Yes, sir.

Senator SMITH. Did you send any messages after that to the Titanic?

Mr. COTTAM. Yes, sir.

Senator SMITH. For whom?

Mr. COTTAM. For the Titanic.

Senator SMITH. At the instance of the captain?

Mr. COTTAM. Yes, sir.

Senator SMITH. What messages?

Mr. COTTAM. Our position.

Senator SMITH. What did you say?

Mr. COTTAM. I simply sent him our position.

Senator SMITH. Can you state it to the reporter?

Mr. COTTAM. I can not remember what the position was now.

Senator SMITH. You can not remember it?

Mr. COTTAM. No, sir.

Senator SMITH. But you gave the position of your ship, its longitude; is that the idea?

Mr. COTTAM. Yes, sir.

Senator SMITH. And you did that at the suggestion of the captain?

Mr. COTTAM. Yes, sir.

Senator SMITH. Did he write out a formal message for you?

Mr. COTTAM. No, sir.

Senator SMITH. He told you?

Mr. COTTAM. Yes, sir.

Senator SMITH. And you sent it?

Mr. COTTAM. Yes, sir; he wrote the position out on a little slip of paper.

Senator SMITH. And you sent that?

Mr. COTTAM. Yes, sir.

Senator SMITH. Did you get any reply to that?

Mr. COTTAM. Yes, sir.

Senator SMITH. How long afterwards?

Mr. COTTAM. Immediately, sir.

Senator SMITH. Signed by anyone?

Mr. COTTAM. No, sir.

Senator SMITH. What did it say?

Mr. COTTAM. It simply gave me "Received."

Senator SMITH. Is that all?

Mr. COTTAM. Yes, sir.

Senator SMITH. Signed by the operator or signed by anybody?

Mr. COTTAM. No, sir.

Senator SMITH. When did you next hear from the Titanic, or communicate with her?

Mr. COTTAM. About four minutes afterwards.

Senator SMITH. Did you communicate with her, or she with you?

Mr. COTTAM: We communicated with each other.

Senator SMITH. Who sent the first message?

Mr. COTTAM. I did.

Senator SMITH. Four minutes after this last message giving your position?

Mr. COTTAM. Yes, sir.

Senator SMITH. You sent another?

Mr. COTTAM. Yes.

Senator SMITH. What did you say in that?

Mr. COTTAM. Confirmed both positions, that of the Titanic and ours.

Senator SMITH. Did you get anything back from that?

Mr. COTTAM. No, sir; only an acknowledgment.

Senator SMITH. What did it say?

Mr. COTTAM. "All right."

Senator SMITH. When did you next communicate or receive a communication?

Mr. COTTAM. A few minutes afterwards.

Senator SMITH. How many minutes?

Mr. COTTAM. I could not say, sir, because there was another ship calling the Titanic.

Senator SMITH. How do you know?

Mr. COTTAM. Because I heard it.

Senator SMITH. What did you hear?

Mr. COTTAM.   I heard him calling the Titanic.

Senator SMITH.   I understand, but what was said?

Mr. COTTAM.   There was nothing but the call, sir.

Senator SMITH.   A distress call?

Mr. COTTAM.   No, sir.

Senator SMITH.   Do you know what boat it was?

Mr. COTTAM.   The Frankfurt.

Senator SMITH.   A North German Lloyd boat?

Mr. COTTAM: I do not know whether it is the North German Lloyd. It is some German line; I do not know which one.

Senator SMITH.   You heard this call?

Mr. COTTAM: Yes.

Senator SMITH.   The German boat was calling the Titanic?

Mr. COTTAM.   Yes, sir.

Senator SMITH.   And did that disarrange your signals?

Mr. COTTAM.   No, sir.

Senator SMITH.   But after that call was finished, then what did you get, if anything?

Mr. COTTAM.   I heard the Olympic calling the Titanic.

Senator SMITH.   Did you hear the Titanic calling the Olympic?

Mr. COTTAM.   No, sir; not at first.

Senator SMITH.   But you heard the Olympic calling the Titanic?

Mr. COTTAM: Yes, sir.

Senator SMITH.   What did the Olympic say?

Mr. COTTAM: He was calling him and offering a service message.

Senator SMITH.   Offering their service?

Mr. COTTAM.   Offering a service message.

Senator SMITH. Offering a service message?

Mr. COTTAM. Yes.

Senator SMITH. Then what followed?

Mr. COTTAM. Nothing, for about a half a minute. Everything was quiet.

Senator SMITH. Nothing for about half a minute?

Mr. COTTAM: Yes.

Senator SMITH. By this time you were quite alert to the situation, were you?

Mr. COTTAM. Yes.

Senator SMITH. Is that right?

Mr. COTTAM. Yes.

Senator SMITH. After this minute, then what?

Mr. COTTAM. I asked the Titanic if he was aware that the Olympic was calling him, sir.

Senator SMITH. What was the reply?

Mr. COTTAM. He said he was not.

Senator SMITH. He was not aware of it?

Mr. COTTAM. No, sir.

Senator SMITH. Then what followed?

Mr. COTTAM. He told me he could not read him because the rush of air and the escape of steam.

Senator SMITH. That he could not read him?

Mr. COTTAM. That he could not read him; yes, sir.

Senator SMITH. Could not read what?

Mr. COTTAM. The Olympic.

Senator SMITH. That he could not read the message from the Olympic because of the rush of air?

Mr. COTTAM. Yes, sir.

Senator SMITH. And the escape of steam?

Mr. COTTAM. Yes, sir.

Senator SMITH. What was the next thing you heard?

Mr. COTTAM. Then the Titanic called the Olympic.

Senator SMITH. Was there anything urgent about that or anything related to the Titanic?

Mr. COTTAM. No, sir.

Senator SMITH. What did you do then?

Mr. COTTAM. I told the Titanic to call the Baltic.

Senator SMITH. What followed?

Mr. COTTAM. The communication was apparently unsatisfactory.

Senator SMITH. It was apparently unsatisfactory?

Mr. COTTAM. Yes.

Senator SMITH. Well, go right ahead and tell us just what occurred as long as you were aboard that ship doing work to the time of the rescue of these people.

Mr. COTTAM. I was in communication at regular intervals the whole of the time until the last communication gained with the Titanic.

Senator SMITH. You heard that?

Mr. COTTAM. Yes, sir.

Senator SMITH. What was said in that message?

Mr. COTTAM. He told him to come at once; that he was head down. And he sent his position.

Senator SMITH. And do you know whether he got any reply to that message?

Mr. COTTAM. Yes, sir.

Senator SMITH. What was it?

Mr. COTTAM. "Received." He told him the message was received.

Senator SMITH. Is that all?

Mr. COTTAM. Yes, sir.

Senator SMITH. When did you hear anything again? What happened next?

Mr. COTTAM. I heard the Baltic calling Cape Race [Newfoundland].

Senator SMITH. You were in regular communication?

Mr. COTTAM. Yes, sir.

Senator SMITH. With the Titanic?

Mr. COTTAM. Yes, sir.

Senator SMITH. Until the last communication was heard?

Mr. COTTAM. Yes; until the last communication was heard.

Senator SMITH. What was the last one?

Mr. COTTAM. The last one was, "Come quick; our engine room is filling up to the boilers."

Senator SMITH. That was the last communication you received?

Mr. COTTAM. Yes, sir.

Senator SMITH. Did you make any reply to it?

Mr. COTTAM. I acknowledged the message and reported it to the captain.

Senator SMITH. Did you report each of those messages to the captain?

Mr. COTTAM. Yes, sir.

Senator SMITH. By leaving your place?

Mr. COTTAM. Yes, sir.

Senator SMITH. And going forward?

Mr. COTTAM. Yes, sir.

Senator SMITH. Or by the captain coming to your room?

208

Mr. COTTAM. No, sir; I reported on the bridge to the captain.

Senator SMITH. And this was the last communication you received?

Mr. COTTAM. Yes, sir.

Senator SMITH. And the reply that was made was to what effect?

Mr. COTTAM. I simply acknowledged the message and went up to the captain and reported it.

Senator SMITH. Was any other message sent to them?

Mr. COTTAM. No, sir.

Senator SMITH. In saying that you acknowledged the message, you just use the word "received"?

Mr. COTTAM. No, sir; we called the Titanic by the three-letter code and signed it by our own and gave the signal for "received" - "R. D."

Senator SMITH. That indicates that the message has been received? Does it indicate any more than that; that it has had attention?

Mr. COTTAM. No, sir.

Senator SMITH. So that in response to this last call the only reply they got was "received"?

Mr. COTTAM. Yes, sir.

Senator SMITH. But the position of your boat was not stated?

Mr. COTTAM. No, sir.

Senator SMITH. I thought I understood the captain to say that one of the last messages told the sinking ship that they were within a certain distance and coming hard, or coming fast.

Mr. COTTAM.   I called him with that message, but I got no acknowledgment.

Senator SMITH.   Just tell us what that message was. You called him with that message?

Mr. COTTAM. Yes, sir.

Senator SMITH.   We would like to know about that; just tell what it was.

Mr. COTTAM. The captain told me to tell the Titanic that all our boats were ready and we were coming as hard as we could come, with a double watch on in the engine room, and to be prepared, when we got there, with lifeboats. I got no acknowledgment of that message.

Senator SMITH. But you sent it?

Mr. COTTAM. Yes, sir.

Senator SMITH. Whether it was received or not, you don't know?

Mr. COTTAM. No, sir.

Senator SMITH.   Let us understand. When you received that last call from the Titanic, that her engine room was filling with water, you say you acknowledged its receipt and took that message to the captain. Did you acknowledge its receipt before you took it to the captain?

Mr. COTTAM. Yes, sir.

Senator SMITH. Then, after you had taken this message to the captain, you came back to your instrument and sent the message that you have just described?

Mr. COTTAM. Yes, sir.

Senator SMITH. And to that you received no reply?

Mr. COTTAM. No, sir.

Senator SMITH. And you never received any other reply?

Mr. COTTAM. No, sir.

Senator SMITH. Or any other word from the ship?

Mr. COTTAM. No, sir.

Senator SMITH. After the Carpathia had picked up these lifeboats and started for New York, did you receive messages?

Mr. COTTAM. Yes, sir.

Senator SMITH. How long did you remain at your post that night?

Mr. COTTAM. All the night, sir.

Senator SMITH. How much of the time next day?

Mr. COTTAM. All the day, sir.

Senator SMITH. That was Sunday and Monday; how about Monday night?

Mr. COTTAM. I was on all night again, sir.

Senator SMITH. And Tuesday?

Mr. COTTAM. All the time again.

Senator SMITH. And Tuesday night?

Mr. COTTAM. I got about a couple or three hours sleep.

Senator SMITH. You got about two or three hours sleep Tuesday night?

Mr. COTTAM. Yes.

Senator SMITH. At what hour?

Mr. COTTAM. I can not say the hour I fell off.

Senator SMITH. You fell off to sleep?

Mr. COTTAM. Yes, sir.

Senator SMITH. Involuntarily?

Mr. COTTAM. Yes, sir.

Senator SMITH. You do not know what time it was?

Mr. COTTAM. No, sir.

Senator SMITH. Or how much you slept?

Mr. COTTAM. No, sir.

Senator SMITH. How were you awakened?

Mr. COTTAM. I don't know, sir.

Senator SMITH. When were you awakened?

Mr. COTTAM. About 20 to half past 4, ship's time, just as the dawn was coming on; about half past 4 in the morning.

Senator SMITH. It was nearing dawn?

Mr. COTTAM. Yes, sir.

Senator SMITH. That would be Wednesday morning?

Mr. COTTAM. Yes, sir.

Senator SMITH. Were you at your post all day Wednesday?

Mr. COTTAM. Yes, sir; with the exception of meals.

Senator SMITH. And Wednesday night?

Mr. COTTAM. Yes, sir; the junior man of the Titanic had then been brought up out of the hospital to give me a hand for a while with the wireless.

Senator SMITH What was your state of mind or physical condition at that time when you got this relief?

Mr. COTTAM. I was feeling very tired, and about worked out.

Senator SMITH. How long did this relief that you got from the Titanic operator continue?

Mr. COTTAM. He gave me a hand all the way to New York.

Senator SMITH. All the way to New York?

Mr. COTTAM. Yes, sir.

Senator SMITH. During those days beginning with Monday morning, was there an attempt made to communicate with your ship often?

Mr. COTTAM. Yes, sir.

Senator SMITH. That was successful?

Mr. COTTAM. Yes, sir.

Senator SMITH. Of course you would not know whether any attempt were made that was not successful?

Mr. COTTAM. No, sir.

Senator SMITH. In other words you have no means of knowing what passed through the air except as it has registered on you instrument?

Mr. COTTAM. No, sir.

Senator SMITH. Was there any successful attempt made to communicate with you on Monday? Did you take any messages on Monday?

Mr. COTTAM. I can not remember that I did on Monday.

Senator SMITH. Can you remember what you did Tuesday?

Mr. COTTAM. I kept no record of the whole work; only memorized it.

Senator SMITH. You kept no record of it?

Mr. COTTAM. No, sir.

Senator SMITH. Was there no written record of those messages?

Mr. COTTAM. Yes, sir.

Senator SMITH. When was it made up?

Mr. COTTAM. As the messages were sent.

Senator SMITH. And received?

Mr. COTTAM. And received.

Senator SMITH. So that those are on file with your ship's office?

Mr. COTTAM. They are in the Marconi house on the ship, sir.

Senator SMITH. Was anybody successful in getting into communication with your ship on Monday and Tuesday?

Mr. COTTAM. I was in communication with some station or other the whole way from the time of the wreck right to New York.

Senator SMITH. You were in communication with some ship?

Mr. COTTAM. Yes, sir.

Senator SMITH. All the way?

Mr. COTTAM: Yes, sir.

Senator SMITH. All the way?

Mr. COTTAM. Yes, sir.

Senator SMITH. And often?

Mr. COTTAM. Yes, sir.

Senator SMITH. Do you recall having received any message from the President of the United States?

Mr. COTTAM. No, sir; I do not remember anything about that.

Senator SMITH. Do you recall getting into communication with either the Chester or the Salem?

Mr. COTTAM. With the Chester, sir.

Senator SMITH. The Chester?

Mr. COTTAM. Yes, sir.

Senator SMITH. What was the nature of their inquiry?

Mr. COTTAM. They were asking for a list of the passengers and crew.

Senator SMITH. Did you comply with their request?

Mr. COTTAM. I asked the captain. The names of the first and second class passengers and the crew had been sent off previously.

Senator SMITH. They had been sent to whom?

Mr. COTTAM. The names of the first and second class passengers had been sent to the Olympic, and the list of the crew had been sent to the Minnewaska.

Senator SMITH. And therefore you did not duplicate those lists?

Mr. COTTAM. No, sir.

Senator SMITH. Was there any message from the Chester?

Mr. COTTAM. They sent some message, but I can not remember whether they were replied to or not. The first message was replied to.

Senator SMITH. Did this wireless instrument or equipment work satisfactorily, so far as you know?

Mr. COTTAM. On the Carpathia?

Senator SMITH. On the Carpathia.

Mr. COTTAM. Yes. It worked satisfactorily for what it was, sir.

Senator SMITH. Did it seem to be an impaired equipment?

Mr. COTTAM. An old type.

Mr. UHLER. What does he mean by that - that the field was limited or the type of machine?

Senator SMITH. The type of machine.

Mr. COTTAM. The type of machine. Both the field of communication and the type of machine.

Mr. UHLER. Both were unsatisfactory?

Mr. COTTAM. Yes, sir.

Senator SMITH. The field was limited by the type, was it not?

Mr. COTTAM. Yes, sir.

Mr. UHLER. What was the power of the machine on the Carpathia?

Senator SMITH. Answer the question. What was the power? What wave length was used?

Mr. UHLER. No; what was the kilowatt?

Senator SMITH. What power did you use?

Mr. COTTAM. I can not tell you the kilowatt; it varied according to the source of supply from the ship's main.

Senator SMITH. I think I will just let you stand aside for a while, but we may want you in the morning; will you be here?

Mr. COTTAM. Yes, sir.

Senator SMITH. I should like to have you here as early as 10 o'clock to-morrow morning.

Mr. GRIGGS. Shall we try to bring down the junior operator of the Titanic at the same time?

Senator SMITH. I wish you would.

Mr. GRIGGS. We will have him here in the morning.

Senator SMITH. Thank you.

Do you know what time you received the message from the Chester?

Mr. COTTAM. That is hard to say, sir, but it would be about half past 9 to 10 o'clock in the morning.

Senator SMITH. Which morning? Tuesday morning?

Mr. COTTAM. Tuesday morning.

Senator SMITH. About half past 9?

Mr. COTTAM. Yes, sir.

Senator SMITH. That is all from you to-night. I will now call Mr. Crawford.

TESTIMONY OF ALFRED CRAWFORD.

Bedroom Steward, SS Titanic

The witness was duly sworn by the chairman.

Senator SMITH. What is your full name?

Mr. CRAWFORD. Alfred Crawford.

Senator SMITH. And where do you reside?

Mr. CRAWFORD. In Southampton.

Senator SMITH. England?

Mr. CRAWFORD. England; yes, sir.

Senator SMITH. How old are you?

Mr. CRAWFORD. Forty-one.

Senator SMITH. What is your business or occupation?

Mr. CRAWFORD. Bedroom steward.

Senator SMITH. How long have you been engaged in that employment?

Mr. CRAWFORD. I have been going to sea since 1881, sir.

Senator SMITH. How long have you been employed on the White Star Line?

Mr. CRAWFORD. I have been on the White Star Line six years.

Senator SMITH. What boats have you served on?

Mr. CRAWFORD. On the Adriatic, the Olympic, and the Titanic.

Senator SMITH. Always in the same capacity?

Mr. CRAWFORD. Yes, sir.

Senator SMITH. What are your duties?

Mr. CRAWFORD.   Attending to all the passengers requirements, cleaning their rooms and everything, sir.

Senator SMITH.   In any particular part of the ship?

Mr. CRAWFORD.   Yes, sir; in one certain part. I was on B deck, right forward.

Senator SMITH.   That is where?

Mr. CRAWFORD.   In the fore part of the ship; in the bow part.

Senator SMITH.   That is on the second from the boat deck?

Mr. CRAWFORD.   The second from the boat deck; yes, sir.

Senator SMITH.   Forward?

Mr. CRAWFORD.   Yes, sir.

Senator SMITH.   Do you know any of the passengers in your part of this ship?

Mr. CRAWFORD.   I know three ladies, Mrs. Rogers, Miss Rogers, and her niece; also Mr. Stewart, that I had in my section, and there was a Mr. And Mrs. Bishop.

Senator SMITH.   Mr. and Mrs. Bishop?

Mr. CRAWFORD.   Yes, sir.

Senator SMITH.   Do you remember Mr. Bishop's initials?

Mr. CRAWFORD.   No; I do not know what were his initials.

Senator SMITH.   Were those all?

Mr. CRAWFORD.   They were a newly married couple.

Senator SMITH.   The Bishops?

Mr. CRAWFORD.   Yes.

Senator SMITH.   He was a man about your age?

Mr. CRAWFORD.   No; he was a man about 24, sir.

Senator SMITH.   A young man.

Mr. CRAWFORD.   A young man; yes, sir.

Senator SMITH. Were these all passengers in your section?

Mr. CRAWFORD. All I had in my section. There were some other passengers up there.

Senator SMITH. Do you remember them?

Mr. CRAWFORD. I do not remember their names, sir.

Senator SMITH. Did you know Mr. and Mrs. Straus?

Mr. CRAWFORD. I stood at the boat where they refused to get in.

Senator SMITH. Did Mrs. Straus get into the boat?

Mr. CRAWFORD. She attempted to get into the boat first and she got back again. Her maid got into the boat.

Senator SMITH. What do you mean by "she attempted" to get in?

Mr. CRAWFORD. She went to get over from the deck to the boat, but then went back to her husband.

Senator SMITH. Did she step on the boat?

Mr. CRAWFORD. She stepped on to the boat, on to the gunwales sir; then she went back.

Senator SMITH. What followed?

Mr. CRAWFORD. She said, "We have been living together for many years, and where you go I go."

Senator SMITH. To whom did she speak?

Mr. CRAWFORD. To her husband.

Senator SMITH. Was he beside her?

Mr. CRAWFORD. Yes; he was standing away back when she went from the boat.

Senator SMITH. You say there was a maid there also?

Mr. CRAWFORD. A maid got in the boat and was saved; yes, sir.

Senator SMITH. Did the maid precede Mrs. Straus into the boat?

Mr. CRAWFORD. Mrs. Straus told the maid to get into the boat and she would follow her; then she altered her mind and went back to her husband.

Senator SMITH. Which one of the boats was that?

Mr. CRAWFORD. No. 8, on the port side.

Senator SMITH. You mean the eighth boat to be lowered?

Mr. CRAWFORD. No, sir; the starboard boats were lowered before ours were. We were on the port side; No.8 boat, on the port side.

Senator SMITH. Who superintended the loading?

Mr. CRAWFORD. The chief officer superintended it, and myself.

Senator SMITH. And the lowering?

Mr. CRAWFORD. And Capt. Smith.

Senator SMITH. All those lifeboats on the port side?

Mr. CRAWFORD. Capt. Smith and the chief officer; Capt. Smith and the steward lowered the forward falls of the boat I was in.

Senator SMITH. This was forward?

Mr. CRAWFORD. Yes, sir.

Senator SMITH. How far from the bridge?

Mr. BURLINGHAM. He said the forward falls, Senator; that is the forward rope, but it was the after boat on the port side.

Senator SMITH. How far from the bridge?

Mr. CRAWFORD. It was about 20 or 30 yards from the bridge, sir.

Senator SMITH. And the captain of the boat personally superintended the loading and the lowering?

Mr. CRAWFORD. Of that one particular boat; yes, sir.

Senator SMITH. Of this eighth boat?

Mr. CRAWFORD. Of No. 8 boat; yes, sir.

Senator SMITH. Did he superintend the loading and lowering of any other boat there forward?

Mr. CRAWFORD. I think he went to No. 10 boat. I could not see that being lowered into the water. He gave us instructions to pull to a light that he saw and then land the ladies and return back to the ship again. It was the light of a vessel in the distance. We pulled and pulled, but we could not reach it.

Senator SMITH. Then you didn't get back to the ship?

Mr. CRAWFORD. No, sir.

Senator SMITH. Where was the captain when you saw him last?

Mr. CRAWFORD. He stood up on the deck there, where we were lowering away the falls. After we got from the boat deck I could not see him again.

Senator SMITH. After you got below the boat deck?

Mr. CRAWFORD. Yes.

Senator SMITH. He remained on the boat deck?

Mr. CRAWFORD. Yes; sir.

Senator SMITH. How many seamen or men of the crew were put into boat No. 8?

Mr. CRAWFORD. Four, sir; two were in and Capt. Smith told me to get in.

Senator SMITH. Two were in?

Mr. CRAWFORD. Two sailors were in the boat at first.

Senator SMITH. And Capt. Smith told you to get in?

Mr. CRAWFORD. Yes, sir; myself and a cook got in. We were the last to get in the boat - there were so many ladies that there wasn't room for any more.

Senator SMITH. How many passengers were in that boat?

Mr. CRAWFORD. I should say about 35, sir.

Senator SMITH. Was that a regular lifeboat or one of these canvas collapsible boats?

Mr. CRAWFORD. No, sir, it was a regular lifeboat.

Senator SMITH. When you were lowered to the water, who assumed charge of this lifeboat?

Mr. CRAWFORD. The man in the afterpart of the lifeboat, a sailor.

Senator SMITH. A sailor?

Mr. CRAWFORD. Yes, sir.

Senator SMITH. And what was done?

Mr. CRAWFORD. We all took an oar and pulled away from the ship. A lady - I don't know her name - took the tiller.

Senator SMITH. A lady took the tiller and the men took the oars?

Mr. CRAWFORD. Four men took the oars and pulled away,

Senator SMITH. Did you know any of the women or men in that boat?

Mr. CRAWFORD. No, sir; there were only ladies. There were no men, except four of the crew.

Senator SMITH. What about Mr. and Mrs. Bishop?

Mr. CRAWFORD. They weren't in that boat.

Senator SMITH. What boat were they in?

Mr. CRAWFORD. I couldn't say what boat they got into. I saw them afterwards on the Carpathia.

Senator SMITH. Did each of the boats forward on the port side have four men?

Mr. CRAWFORD. I think they did, sir, I couldn't say. I was out loading all the boats as we got along.

Senator SMITH. So far as you observed, was there any struggle -

Mr. CRAWFORD. No, sir; none whatever.

Senator SMITH. (continuing): To get into the lifeboats, by men or women?

Mr. CRAWFORD. No, sir; none whatever.

Senator SMITH. Was the ship sinking at this time?

Mr. CRAWFORD. She was making water fast at the bows; yes, sir.

Senator SMITH. And was there any noticeable suction?

Mr. CRAWFORD. No, sir.

Senator SMITH. About the boat?

Mr. CRAWFORD. No, sir; I do not think so.

Senator SMITH. As she began to sink?

Mr. CRAWFORD. No, sir.

Senator SMITH. Just tell what you did from that time that you were lowered to the water.

Mr. CRAWFORD. Kept pulling and trying to make a light, and we could not seem to get any closer to it. We kept pulling and pulling until daybreak. Then we saw the Carpathia coming up, and we turned around and came back to her.

Senator SMITH. What time did the day break on Monday?

Mr. CRAWFORD. About 4 o'clock, I should say, it began to get light.

Senator SMITH. You were in the boat and pulling?

Mr. CRAWFORD: Yes, sir; until the time we were picked up.

Senator SMITH. From 1 o'clock until about daylight?

Mr. CRAWFORD. Yes, sir.

Senator SMITH. When you were picked up, did the boat have the same number of occupants as when she left the Titanic?

Mr. CRAWFORD. Yes, sir.

Senator SMITH. And all were saved?

Mr. CRAWFORD. And all were saved; yes, sir.

Senator SMITH. Where were you when this collision occurred?

Mr. CRAWFORD. I was right forward in B deck.

Senator SMITH. Where is that?

Mr. CRAWFORD. Two decks underneath the boat deck.

Senator SMITH. Tell what you experienced.

Mr. CRAWFORD. I was on watch until 12 o'clock, and I was waiting for my relief to come up. I was to be relieved at 12 o'clock. I heard the crash, and I went out on the outer deck and saw the iceberg floating alongside. I went back, and there were a lot of passengers coming out.

Senator SMITH. You went out on the outer deck?

Mr. CRAWFORD. Yes, sir.

Senator SMITH. On which side?

Mr. CRAWFORD. On the starboard side.

Senator SMITH. And saw the iceberg?

Mr. CRAWFORD. I saw the iceberg going by.

Senator SMITH. Was there any ice on the deck?

Mr. CRAWFORD. I did not go so far forward as that, sir.

Senator: SMITH: Was there anybody injured that you know anything about?

Mr. CRAWFORD.   No, sir, I went to all the ladies' cabins. They were all rushing out, and I told them I didn't think there was any immediate danger, and after the order was passed for the life belts, I tied the life belts on the ladies, and an old gentleman by the name of Stewart, and tied his shoes on for him.

Senator SMITH. You say after the order was passed for the life belts?

Mr. CRAWFORD. Yes.

Senator SMITH. Who gave that order?

Mr. CRAWFORD. The captain, I believe.

Senator SMITH. How long after the collision?

Mr. CRAWFORD. I should say about 30 minutes.

Senator SMITH. Did you succeed in getting the life belts on?

Mr. CRAWFORD.   On all the ladies, and all the passengers; yes, sir.

Senator SMITH. On all passengers you say?

Mr. CRAWFORD. Yes, sir; all that were on that deck.

Senator SMITH.   Did you personally look after the passengers on that deck in that regard?

Mr. CRAWFORD. Yes, sir.

Senator SMITH. Did anybody assist you?

Mr. CRAWFORD.   There was another man on the other side. There was one man on each side.

Senator SMITH. You say that all the passengers were fitted with lifebelts?

Mr. CRAWFORD.   Yes, sir; each person. There were three or four life belts in each stateroom.

Senator SMITH. Were there any children on that deck?

Mr. CRAWFORD. No, sir; there was none on the deck where I was.

Senator SMITH. Did you know any of the other passengers on that deck?

Mr. CRAWFORD. No, sir; I could not say that I did.

Senator SMITH. Did you hear of any American passengers there?

Mr. CRAWFORD. No.

Senator SMITH. On that deck?

Mr. CRAWFORD. No, sir.

Senator SMITH. I mean by that, any special names that were suggested?

Mr. CRAWFORD. No, sir; I have not heard of any.

Senator SMITH. Those people you have enumerated are the only ones you know by name?

Mr. CRAWFORD. That is all; yes, sir.

Senator SMITH. Did you hear any explosion or any evidence of an explosion?

Mr. CRAWFORD. I heard an explosion when we were lying to in the water, in the boat, sir.

Senator SMITH. In what boat?

Mr. CRAWFORD. In the lifeboat.

Senator SMITH. What character of explosion?

Mr. CRAWFORD. Sort of a sharp, like as if there were things being blown up.

Senator SMITH. Was there any outward indication?

Mr. CRAWFORD. No, sir; we did not see any, because we were pulling very hard away.

Senator SMITH. Did you see the ship go down?

Mr. CRAWFORD. We saw her at a distance; yes, sir.

Senator SMITH. What shape was she in when you saw her last?

Mr. CRAWFORD. It seemed as if her bow was going down first.

Senator SMITH. At how much of an angle?

Mr. CRAWFORD. We saw all the lights going out on the forward part of her.

Senator SMITH. And still burning on the after part?

Mr. CRAWFORD. Yes, sir.

Senator SMITH. How much of the after part was out of the water?

Mr. CRAWFORD. There was a good bit of the stern part out of water.

Senator SMITH. How many decks?

Mr. CRAWFORD. I could not say how many decks there, sir, but it seemed all clear right from amidships to aft.

Senator SMITH. Did you see many people?

Mr. CRAWFORD. I saw a great number on deck.

Senator SMITH. On board of her at that time.

Mr. CRAWFORD. Yes, sir.

Senator SMITH. What were they doing?

Mr. CRAWFORD. When we left they were trying to lower the other boats; the farther aft boats.

Senator SMITH. Were you assisted in rowing the boat that you were in by a woman pulling an oar?

CRAWFORD. Yes, sir.

Senator SMITH. Who was she?

Mr. CRAWFORD. I don't know her name, sir. There were several there who took turns at pulling.

Senator SMITH. Were they employees?

Mr. CRAWFORD. No, sir.

Senator SMITH. They were lady passengers?

Mr. CRAWFORD. Yes, sir; lady passengers.

Senator SMITH. But you don't know who they were?

Mr. CRAWFORD. No, sir.

Senator SMITH. You have never seen them since?

Mr. CRAWFORD. No, sir; I have never seen them since.

Senator SMITH. Did you know Mr. Ismay - the managing director?

Mr. CRAWFORD. Yes, sir.

Senator SMITH. Did you see him there?

Mr. CRAWFORD. Yes, sir; I saw him lowering a boat on the starboard side too, and Mr. Murdoch.

Senator SMITH. He and Mr. Murdoch?

Mr. CRAWFORD. Yes, sir.

Senator SMITH. Do you remember what boat it was?

Mr. CRAWFORD. I think it was No. 5.

Senator SMITH. Forward.

Mr. CRAWFORD. Yes, sir; it was just under the bridge.

Senator SMITH. In their order of being lowered into the water, what number was it?

Mr. CRAWFORD. The boat, sir?

Senator SMITH. Yes.

Mr. CRAWFORD. No. 5, starboard side.

Senator SMITH. Was it the fifth boat that was lowered into the water?

Mr. CRAWFORD. Yes, sir; probably the third.

Senator SMITH. Did you see him lowering any other boat?

Mr. CRAWFORD. No; I went around the port side.

Senator SMITH. Did you see him get into a boat?

Mr. CRAWFORD. No, sir.

Senator SMITH. Or get out of one?

Mr. CRAWFORD. No, sir; I saw him assisting the ladies into this one particular boat; he and Mr. Murdoch had lowered the boat into the water.

Senator SMITH. You saw him assist the ladies in?

Mr. CRAWFORD. Yes, sir.

Senator SMITH. Does it take two men to lower the boats?

Mr. CRAWFORD. Yes, sir.

Senator SMITH. And he was performing the service of one man?

Mr. CRAWFORD. Mr. Murdoch was running it through the blocks.

Senator SMITH. And Mr. Murdoch's position was what?

Mr. CRAWFORD. First officer.

Senator SMITH. Did he survive?

Mr. CRAWFORD. No, sir.

Senator SMITH. Either before you got into this lifeboat or after you got into it, did you see many persons in the water?

Mr. CRAWFORD. No, sir.

Senator SMITH. How many?

Mr. CRAWFORD. I did not see any in the water after we lowered the boats.

Senator SMITH. You did not?

Mr. CRAWFORD. No, sir.

Senator SMITH. Did you see any in the water before you lowered the boat?

Mr. CRAWFORD. No, sir.

Senator SMITH. Do you know the condition of these lifeboats?

Mr. CRAWFORD. The one I was in was in very good condition.

Senator SMITH. Was it new?

Mr. CRAWFORD. Yes, sir; and perfectly dry.

Senator SMITH. Was there any difficulty in lowering the lifeboats?

Mr. CRAWFORD. None whatever, sir. They went down very easily.

Senator SMITH. After the captain told you to get into this boat, you did not see him again?

Mr. CRAWFORD. No, sir.

Senator SMITH. Were there any officers in the boat that you were in?

Mr. CRAWFORD. No, sir.

Senator SMITH. Did you see any of the officers get into any boats?

Mr. CRAWFORD. No; I did not, sir.

Senator SMITH. Did you see any attempt made to get into any of the boats?

Mr. CRAWFORD. No, sir.

Senator SMITH. Did you see Mr. Lightoller?

Mr. CRAWFORD. No, sir.

Senator SMITH. Do you know him?

Mr. CRAWFORD. I did not know him; no, sir.

Senator SMITH. You did know Mr. Murdoch?

Mr. CRAWFORD. Yes, sir; I have been with him on several ships.

Senator SMITH. What was your emergency boat station?

Mr. CRAWFORD. No. 8. Each man went to his station.

Senator SMITH. Was that your emergency station?

Mr. CRAWFORD. Yes, sir.

Senator SMITH. What was your fire station?

Mr. CRAWFORD. To get the hose out on each section for the bed rooms.

Senator SMITH. Was there any drill?

Mr. CRAWFORD. Oh, yes; we have a drill every voyage, sir.

Senator SMITH. Did you have any on this voyage?

Mr. CRAWFORD. Yes.

Senator SMITH. When?

Mr. CRAWFORD. That was in Belfast.

Senator SMITH. Before leaving?

Mr. CRAWFORD. Before leaving.

Senator SMITH. Was that at the time of the trial test?

Mr. CRAWFORD. Yes, sir.

Senator SMITH. Who conducted it?

Mr. CRAWFORD. The chief officer, sir.

Senator SMITH. Do you have his name?

Mr. CRAWFORD. Mr. Wilde, sir.

Senator SMITH. I have not finished with you, but I would be glad to have you come here in the morning. We shall not be able to get through with these men.

Mr. BURLINGHAM. Then we will retain them for you. Do you want these 4 officers and these 12 men?

Senator SMITH. Yes.

Mr. BURLINGHAM. The rest can go home?

Senator SMITH. No, I cannot say that.

Mr. BURLINGHAM. We have about 100 of them - 95 stewards and 70 firemen - all prepared to go home by the Lapland; at your service of course, at any time; but that is their home.

Senator SMITH. I understand that; but I am not prepared to meet that request.

Mr. BURLINGHAM. We can not be responsible for their being kept here for you if the ship goes. They are absolutely free from us. They will be subject to boarding houses, or anything else. If the committee wants to herd them up, that is one thing. It is perfectly impossible for a steamship company to take care of 200 people without any steamer to put them on.

Senator SMITH. I am not going to subpoena all of those men. As I understand it, we are to be guaranteed the presence of the officers and these 15 men?

Mr. BURLINGHAM. Yes; those that you have selected.

Senator SMITH. I am not going to release the others.

Mr. BURLINGHAM. But they are not under subpoena.

Senator SMITH. They are not.

Mr. BURLINGHAM. Thank you. We understand, sir.

Senator SMITH. I do not want to release anybody,. and I particularly want these 15.

Mr. BURLINGHAM. They will be here.

Senator SMITH. And the other officers of the company?

Mr. BURLINGHAM. They will be at your disposal to-morrow. At what time?

Senator SMITH. At 10 o'clock.

Mr. BURLINGHAM. Very well, sir.

Senator SMITH. The Sergeant at Arms says there are 12 instead of 15.

Mr. FRANKLIN. Has the Sergeant at Arms the names of the 12 men and the 4 officers?

Senator SMITH. Yes.

Mr. BURLINGHAM. We will have them here. They will be here at 10 o'clock to-morrow morning.